The Dancers' Study Guide

Anthony King

Published by Faria Publishing Limited 2019

The Dancers' Study Guide (First Edition)
© Anthony King, 2019

Edited by Debz Hobbs-Wyatt
Formatted by Polgarus Studio

ISBN: 978-1-9160887-2-6 (print)
ISBN: 978-1-9160887-3-3 (eBook)

Disclaimer: This book is not intended to be a substitute for the medical advice of a licensed physician. The reader should consult with their doctor in any matters relating to his/her health. Before continuing reading this book it is recommended that you seek medical advice from your personal physician and follow their instructions only. The information contained within this book is strictly for informational purposes. If you wish to apply ideas contained in this book, you are taking full responsibility for your actions. The author has made every effort to ensure the accuracy of the information within this book was correct at the time of publication. The author does not assume and hereby disclaims any liability to any party for any loss, damage, or disruption caused by errors or omissions, whether such errors or omissions result from accident, negligence, or any other cause.

I dedicate this book to my dear friends,
Hege and Karsten

Contents

Author's Note

This book incorporates writing from my 2007 book *Dance Like the Stars*. I originally started writing that book as a teenager, already very experienced when it came to the arts. I had been performing and teaching professionally since the age of ten. However, since then I have gone on to teach tens of thousands of people to dance, including celebrities, sports stars, royalty and students; from all around the world. I have taken some of the elements from that book and added some new advice gathered from my experiences. I have noticed that the easiest thing for people to grasp is the physical aspects of most artistic expression. However, it makes no difference if you are rich or poor, powerful or weak, successful or unsuccessful; it's the psychological elements which motivate creative expression before the physical act. I have written a book called *The Personal Development Book For Performers* which takes a close look into these things and helps expressive people (especially the artist or creative person) to excel in their given field. It looks at the simple things; things often not communicated in a class, that are of utmost importance for creative expression. I strongly encourage you not only to focus on your physical expertise and body but also your psychological mind set so that you can reach your full potential and become the best dancer that you can be. You can read all about that in *The Personal Development Book For Performers*, which you can find out more about on my website or at the back of this book.

Introduction

I'm a choreographer and a dance teacher. As you're reading this I'm going to assume that you want to improve your dancing abilities and build your dance knowledge. Welcome! Do with this book as you please. Feel free to take your marker and highlight sections; skip the health bits if you want. Start at the back and work backwards – whatever you feel inclined to do. You are free to pick and choose whatever bits you feel are relevant and helpful for you. Remember, before executing a dance step it is vital that we understand our intention in order to convey that step effectively for others to appreciate and admire. A book or schooling alone is not enough to master a craft. I see dancing as a physical expression of who we are and we can learn to become a better dancer through education, training and personal growth. We will examine what I believe are some of the most important aspects of artistic expression. Firstly in an attempt to understand who we are as individuals and not just dancers; and secondly how to convey who we are to others through the physical movements of dance.

Part 1

Dance History and Basics

The History of Dance

Dance is a physical expression. It's a movement and it exists in a moment of time. Consequently, we cannot accurately date the origins of dance because we don't have the usual evidence (physical proof or artefacts). However, it's a fair supposition that as long as human beings have existed and been able to move – they have danced. We know that dance has been part of human civilisation by way of religious ceremony, ritual and expression since the first humans. We do have ancient Egyptian archaeological evidence, painting and depictions of dance and movement which trace back over 5000 years. The ancient Greeks used dance as part of their religious ceremonies. It was used as both education and entertainment. We also have prehistoric rock painting at The Bhimbetka rock shelters in central India which depicts dancing and ritual, which dates back 30,000 years. We are all aware of how movement and dance were once used as a means of communicating history and as a means of storytelling. In fact, many contemporary and modern forms of dance can be traced back to ancient times, including certain ethnic, ceremonial and traditional dances. It's also important to remember that dance and movement were 'created' before drawing and writing. Oral traditions, which included dance expression came first which helped people pass on their history and culturally important stories to the next generation. These traditions are part of world history and an important part of the development of human civilisation. Dance has always been a method of human interaction, communication and bonding through social interaction.

We can see that dance was an important part of ancient Greece and Rome through its depiction in ancient art and historical writings. The ancient Greek, Orpheus, who is one of the most significant inspirations of the western arts, was a legendary musician, poet and prophet in their religion and myth. He inspired dance and performance for thousands of years and even through to modern times with ballet, in the 1940s from the great Igor Stravinsky. We also see dance being traced back in cultures all over the world, for thousands of years, including the Chinese, Indian and many other traditional forms of dance which evolved into and influenced European traditions. We have seen ceremonial dance performed in the form of religious ritual in Africa through various rites for thousands of years and we even have shamanic dances to elicit rain for the cultivation of crops. In fact, these rituals and rites are still an integral part of their culture and identity. However, this is not only a practice that can be found in Asia or Africa or South America because this kind of folk dance and celebrations can be found in almost all cultures and locations around the world. In Europe, many countries celebrate the harvest with folk dance. These celebrations often centre around the dance element of these religious ceremonies. It's important to differentiate between folk dance and religious dance though because there are important differences depending on the culture and setting. For example, certain dances of 'ritual' are not considered 'folk' dances because the intention behind them is slightly different. They may, however, look very similar. Ironically, the term 'ethnic 'or 'traditional' might be used to describe all types of religious, ceremonial or folk dance, mainly because it is often culturally linked to a certain area or ethnicity.

In Europe, we have many types of folk dance, including:

Barn dance
Clogging
English country dance
Georgian folk dance
Greek dance
Irish dance
Italian folk dance
Maypole dance
Morris dance
Polka
Polish folk dance
Russian folk dance
Turkish dance
Ukrainian dance
Nordic dance
Sword dance

This represents a small part of a much longer list. However, you can see that dance is an important part of our religious and cultural identity. It is, in a sense, our history. The evolution of dance in Europe, through folk and medieval dance, at times is fragmented but it's clear that it was primarily propagated by all classes of people but specifically the upper classes, especially from the Renaissance 15th century, when ballet was actually performed in the royal court, which rose to real prominence in the 17th century during the reign of King Louis XIV. Ballet rose to prominence in France and especially at the world-famous Paris Opera House during the 18th century where the art evolved even further to an actual professional 'performance', with professional dancers, narrative and less costume/masks. It focussed more on the dancers and the dance, rather than the more ballet 'demonstrations' and displays in the various European royal courts.

What is interesting is the new widespread distribution of different dance styles around the world, as well as music, which was helped by the ease of travel and the consequent sharing of culture. This not only helped spread the various artistic styles but helped mix them, which in turn, has created new styles. We then saw an evolution from classical ballet into a more 'contemporary' dance style which moved away from the formal rules of ballet. This modern dance, although based upon classical technique, liked to break the traditional rules. We have also seen the rise of street dance and various styles of dance often promoted by specific artists and celebrities.

The Dancer's Brain

There is scientific evidence that dancing affects the brain in a number of positive ways. These changes might be thought of as a rewiring of some neural pathways. It has been shown that dancers' brains react in different ways to non-dancers' brains. However, it's important to note that these positive effects are not necessarily large. The human brain is optimised, in other words it is highly balanced, to such an extent that if it were significantly physiologically changed in one way, such as through dance, there may be reductions or less positive impacts in other brain areas to compensate.

With all of that said, there were significant differences found. A neuroscientist called Agnieszka Burzynska, from Colorado State University in the United States, investigated the link between dancers and non-dancers' brain activity and published her findings: *The Dancing*

Brain: Structural and Functional Signatures of Expert Dance Training (by Agnieszka Z. Burzynska, Karolina Finch, Brittany K. Taylor, Anya M. Knecht and Arthur F. Kramer) in *Frontiers in Human Neuroscience*, which is according to the publication "a leading journal in its field, publishing rigorously peer-reviewed research that advances our understanding of the brain mechanisms supporting cognitive and social behaviour in humans, in both healthy and diseased states". The article states:

"Dance is a pleasurable and captivating activity that involves motor, cognitive, visuospatial, social, and emotional engagement. Although practised for thousands of years in rituals and as a leisure activity, the long term effects of systematic dance training on cognition and brain structure and function are not well understood."

In her conclusion:

"We showed that dancers' brains differed from non-dancers' at both functional and structural levels".

Although the changes are subtle they are changes nevertheless. Dancers appear to be much better at picking up choreography and dance-related brain activity but this doesn't seem to transfer to a better memory or a 'better' brain, compared to a non-dancer for normal every day actions. You still have the same brain and capacity to remember and forget. It also appears that the brain size is no different either.

The same neuroscientist, Agnieszka Burzynska, was interviewed by Galadriel Watson, who published an article in *Dance* magazine – dancemagazine.com (9th January 2018) who summarised additional findings, including that dancers are better at focussing on dance. Watson said, "When watching a performance, a dancer's brain hops into action, almost as if she were dancing the piece herself."

Muscle Memory and Repetition

It seems intuitively obvious that we become better at things the more we do them. This leads us on to the repetition and muscle memory which is when, according to Diane Solway, in her fascinating *New York Times* piece (May 28th 2007) *How the body (and mind) learns a dance:*

"… movements become thoroughly mapped in the brain, creating a shorthand between thinking and doing."

As dancers, we learn and get better at expressing a dance move by rehearsal, training and repetition. We do so to such an extent that it certainly feels that our mind and brain can switch off; that we enter the 'zone' and allow the body to perform on autopilot. Every dancer or performer will know exactly what this feels like. I also think that it's important to add one further observation omitted from these studies. When in the 'zone', performing a movement that has been seared into your muscle memory, allows your brain to rest. In my experience there seems to be a link between rest and performance. This means that when executing a dance move you don't have to utilise the brain in the same way as when learning the dance. By entering this state of 'zoning out' we allow ourselves to feel more relaxed and in a 'zen' like state. I believe that this state has a beneficial effect on a human being, although this is from personal experience only and not necessarily backed up with scientific evidence. Scientist and talented dancer, Hanna Poikonen, wrote an article entitled *A dancer's brain develops in a unique way* (30th

August 2018) for **helsinki.fi** where she described *"Flow experiences have been found to increase the general contentment and productivity of the person as well as the quality of the activity… has an important role in generating a relaxed state of mind."*

She also wrote:

"The auditory and motor cortex of dancers develops in a unique way. In my study, the dancers' brains reacted more quickly to changes in the music than those of musicians or members of the control group. The change is apparent in the brain as a reflex, before the dancer is even aware of it at a conscious level."

There is a beneficial effect to this experience which Scott Edwards wrote about in his article *Dancing and the Brain* for Harvard Medical School on **neuro.hms.harvard.edu**. Edwards pointed out:

"Dance, in fact, has such beneficial effects on the brain that it is now being used to treat people with Parkinson's disease, a progressive neurological movement disorder."

He then goes on to describe, in the same article, a 2012 study by researchers at North Dakota's

Minot State University, which seemed to show that Zumba, "improves mood and certain cognitive skills, such as visual recognition and decision-making." Edwards also points out that various other studies show that, *"dance helps reduce stress, increases levels of the feel-good hormone serotonin, and helps develop new neural connections, especially in regions involved in executive function, long term memory, and spatial recognition."*

Effects of dance on motor functions, cognitive functions, and mental symptoms of Parkinson's disease, by Hiroko Hashimoto

The study which Edwards refers to was called *Effects of dance on motor functions, cognitive functions, and mental symptoms of Parkinson's disease: A quasi-randomized pilot trial. Complementary Therapies in Medicine*, April 2015 by Hiroko Hashimoto (Hashimoto, Takabatake, Miyaguchi, Nakanishi, Naitou). The studies' objective was "To examine the effectiveness of dance on motor functions, cognitive functions, and mental symptoms of Parkinson's disease (PD)". Forty-six patients participated and it was concluded that:

"Dance was effective in improving motor function, cognitive function, and mental symptoms in PD patients. General symptoms in PD also improved. Dance is an effective method for rehabilitation in PD patients."

Science is certainly catching up with what every dancer already knows: the benefits they feel when they dance and how this helps them in many areas of their life, physically and mentally. Dance has been used as an expression of spirituality and connection to the universe for thousands of years.

Dance Historical Time Line

9000 – 5000 BC Evidence points towards ancient Egyptian, Greek and Indian dance

500 BC Greek Chorus dance

500 AD Belly dance and other cultural dances

1400 – 1500s Maypole folk dance

1400 – 1608 Various court dances

1448 Ballet created and first seen

1581 The first Ballet *Le Ballet Comique de* la Reine is staged

1661 The Académie Royale de Danse (Royal Academy of Ballet), founded by King Louis XIV of France

1770s The waltz

1774 Flamenco dance

1840 Tap dance

1840s Burlesque dance

1840s Polka dance

1880s Tango dance

1900 Jazz dance begins (unrelated to jazz music)

1910s Modern dance

1920s Tap dance

1923 The Charleston

1930s Rumba dance

1934 Jitterbug

1935 Swing

1930s Boogie Woogie

1930 – 1960s Jazz dance evolves

1940s Contemporary dance

1948 New York City Ballet founded

Contemporary dance in the 1950s combined classical ballet with modern dance creating many different new styles including:

1950s Boogaloo

1950s Bop

1950s Rock and Roll

1958 Bossa Nova

1958 Twist

1960s The Frug/Bob Fosse

1960s Locomotion

1960s A kind of 'Postmodern' dance emerged

1967 Hip-hop dance begins

1967 The Robot dance

1960s – 1970s B-boying

1969 Locking

1970s Popping

1970s Waacking (originally called Waack/Punk)
Breaking (early 1970s)

1970s Dancehall (late 1970s)

1975s Disco dance

1980s Backslide (Jeffrey Daniel), MC Hammer
dance, Madonna

1990 Vogue

2000's Krumping

Dance Styles: Overview

Ballet

First created in the 15th century, ballet is probably one of the world's most famous dance styles. It evolved into the ballet we now recognise in the 19th century with its formalised gestures and steps. Its graceful movements often hide the strenuous energy, technique and power required by the dancer which is self-evident when looking at the ballet dancers' physique and a close inspection of their pointe shoes which have reinforced toes, for protection. Ballet is taught worldwide and has influenced the world of performance and art as well as western culture. Its moves are described using French terminology.

Ballroom

The word ballroom (in ballroom dance) actually comes from the Latin word 'ballare', which translates as 'to dance'. The ball 'room' itself is a large room where such dance is performed. Jehan Tabourot (using the pen name hoinot-Arbeau) first described this type of dancing in 1588 in *Orchésographie* which looked at French renaissance social dance. At this time the dance was very much for the privileged classes, as the lower classes were engaged in folk dance and other types of religious movement and ritual. However, over time this has changed with the ballroom dance being one of the most famous styles of dance to participate in and one of the most visual styles, as seen on stage, television and film. The definition of the style is extremely wide but is often described as any partner dance. The waltz is a famous type of ballroom dancing.

Tap Dance

Tap dance is a style of dance where the practitioner uses shoes, often fitted with a special heel and toe (often metal) which creates an audible sound when striking the floor. This creates a percussive sound which is emphasised by the dancer using techniques like syncopation whilst they rhythmically strike the floor with their feet. Tap dance is said to have its ethnic roots in certain

African tribal dances, flamenco (Spain), clog dancing (England) and Irish dance. It's thought to have started off, as we know it, in the mid-1800s during the rise of the 'minstrel' American entertainment shows. Some say it rose to prominence first in the United States and others in the United Kingdom. One of the oldest records of flamenco is from a 1774 book by José Cadalso called *Las Cartas Marruecas*.

Burlesque

The word burlesque is actually defined as "an absurd or comically exaggerated imitation of something, especially in a literary or dramatic work; a parody". The word is derived from the Italian word 'burlesco' which comes from 'burla' – or joke. The word burlesque has been used since the late 17th century in a literary sense, in the English language and later evolved into what we know, primarily through the United States variety show format which was popular from the 1860s to the 1940s. These shows were performed in cabarets, clubs and theatres and sometimes involved a striptease. The 1972 film *Cabaret* helped bring burlesque to a wider audience and it has become more and more popular due to performers like Dita Von Teese. The dance style usually involves a striptease and sexy movements and gestures.

Tango

Tango is a partner dance which originated during the 1880s along the Río de Plata between Argentina and Uruguay. Its style is passionate, playful and uses a lot of improvisation with a leader and a follower. There are many worldwide variations of tango but the original version, according to Wikipedia, was "On August 31, 2009, UNESCO approved a joint proposal by Argentina and Uruguay to include the tango in the UNESCO Intangible Cultural Heritage Lists". The style, at its core is a result of a combination of many other styles including waltz, polka, African candombe, and Argentinian milonga amongst others. Tango is an impulsive dance which is passionate and personal based on individual steps. Its improvised style varies as does tempo and rhythm.

Jazz dance

The dance term 'jazz' has almost no real link to jazz music. It's a word used to describe the incorporation of a wide range of dance styles and techniques. Broadway and Hollywood, since the 1940s, have certainly promoted the style as we now know it with choreographers like Jerome Robbins and Bob Fosse but it usually combines various styles. It originated from African American or Caribbean dance to form a kind of modern jazz dance which emerged in the 1950s. All styles of jazz dance, including theatre jazz or street jazz, for example, will find their roots within both the original African American or Caribbean dance. Jazz dance continues to change and evolve incorporating other styles.

Contemporary dance

Contemporary dance emerged in the 1950s and is now one of the most dominant styles of dance in the world today. It combines ballet, jazz and modern dance but allows trained dancers to focus on unshackling from the rigid rules of ballet which creates a more abstract aesthetic. This is combined with the freedom to express as the choreographer or dancer wishes through often abstract, non-standard and unpredictable movement. The style emerged as experimentation and reaction against ballet's rigid rules but also incorporates it into its style to create often free-flowing movement, by moving the body in an untraditional way compared to ballet training.

Hip-hop dance

Hip-hop dance incorporates a wide range of styles and people from the late 1960s in New York City. This freestyle improvisational style of dance which started off being danced outside (and then later inside dance studios with a commercial/new version of hip-hop) was created by black Americans and Latino Americans. 'Battles' and dance competitions helped spread the style which would be promoted worldwide on television in the 1980s. Hip-hop dance includes: breaking, locking, b-boying, popping and many other styles including pop music and rap music video dance that we see today.

Disco

Disco dance, in my opinion, is one of the styles which has had a big impact on modern-day dance but not in an obvious way because it is based upon the music it is named after. The dance originated in the 1970s in the United States' club scene and was made famous by John Travolta in *Saturday*

Night Fever. The movie soundtrack, featuring the Bee Gees, would go on to become one of the biggest selling albums of all time and have a massive cultural impact. Disco incorporated partner and line dance, solo dance and disco freestyle. In the late 1970s, it developed incorporating styles that remain to this day including 'The robot' and 'boogaloo'. The dance style also incorporated many elements of salsa, funk, samba, cha cha and jazz.

Street dance

Street dance is an umbrella term for a style which incorporates many styles of dance including, locking, popping, house and a variety of urban style moves which literally started in the street and often outside dance studios. Saturday afternoons used to have more dancing outside our dance studio than inside. Street dance is high energy; it is both improvisational and social in nature which depends on exactly where it takes place. For example, New York City propagated breakdancing and b-boying, literally in the street and it was a cultural expression and art. It developed naturally and organically and includes a wide number of styles including locking, funk, waving and krumping amongst others.

Dance Terms: Glossary

8 count

An 8 count is simply eight beats: "One, two, three, four, five, six, seven, eight" and used to measure music and is also used in dance. An 8 count is two 'bars' and a 'bar' is a measure of four beats, as in; "one, two, three, four". Sometimes single bars are used as measurements in dance and are called out and verbally spoken. In music, they are written in notation form. These counts can be extended or joined together. I personally count in counts of four or eight, like this; "**One**, two, three, four, **two**, two, three, four, **three**, two, three four, **four**, two, three, four." This way, I can count four bars and can easily identify and count which bar, as well as the number of bars, whilst verbally communicating a step, dancing a step or thinking about a step.

Adagio

Adagio means slow movement both in music and in dance. It is something which is not fast and in ballet is typically a graceful, easy, slow movement. It comes from the Italian and translates as 'at ease'.

Allegro

Allegro simply means performed at a brisk speed. When this term is applied to dance it means that fast movements and steps are required (a jeté jump for example). It's an Italian word that describes tempo.

Alignment

The Oxford dictionary describes alignment as an "arrangement in a straight line or incorrect relative positions" and a "position of agreement or alliance" and this is exactly the same in dance. The exact alignment depends on your intention but the form you use will include stance and placement of your body, aligned in a way which communicates appropriately.

Allongé

This is a French term which simply means elongated or stretched. You might be asked to elongate your arabesque, for example, by stretching out your leg further.

Arabesque

An arabesque is a ballet position where your leg is extended behind your body, whilst your supporting leg can be either straight or in plié (bent). The non-supporting leg is fully extended and straight. It is one of the most famous dance steps in ballet.

Assemblé

Assemblé or pas assemblé essentially translates from the French as 'step put together' and is executed in a variety of ways. It describes a movement when your legs join together in the air and you land on both feet. Your leg will slide across the floor before the jump, in its basic form.

Arch

This depends on your style of dance but is essentially where you use your body to create an arch by extending your upper body (or whole body).

Attitude

An attitude is a ballet position which is actually inspired by a statue of the god Mercury, according to Carlo Blasis in 1829 (*Encyclopaedia Britannica*). An attitude is very similar to an arabesque, except that the knee is bent (in the raised leg) and the leg can be raised towards the front or the back.

Ballerina and Ballerino

The term ballerina is often used to describe a female ballet dancer, however, this title was only historically given to the highest ranking principle dancer. The star male dancer is called a ballerino as are often male ballet dancers.

Barre

The barre is a wooden (or metal) handrail bar that is attached (or sometimes free-standing) to the wall in a dance studio or rehearsal room. Dancers utilise it for stretching and to use as support whilst engaging in exercises. These exercises are often called 'barre work'. The height of the bar varies but is usually approximately one metre (100 cm).

Beat

The beat is a measurement of time, as described above in '8 counts'. One count is usually one beat (but not always). The beat is the pulse of the piece which you can count out, like "one, two, three, four" which each number, in this one bar example being one beat. The beat can also be used to describe the drum and percussion sounds and tempo of a piece.

Ball Change

A ball change is simply a move which involves the change of weight from one foot to the other and a kind of stepping action. A kick ball change is the same but starting off with a kick.

Bass

The bass is the lowest of the four standard voice ranges: soprano, alto, tenor and bass. Musically it is the low (or deep) sounds with frequencies ranging from 16 to 256 Hz. When we dance we can often feel the bass and it usually helps drive a piece of music and the dance.

Chassé

The word chassé, from the French means *to chase* and the ballet dance step is reminiscent of a kind of gallop. It is a basic step of ballet where the front foot extends forward and is chased by the back foot, all in a forward motion.

Choreographer

It is the composer who composes music and it is the choreographer who creates dance steps, dance moves and choreography. Sometimes a choreographer will be a kind of conductor, director or orchestrator which means that they do not always conceive original choreography but can still be classed as a choreographer.

Choreography

Choreography is the term we use to describe the actual dance moves and dance steps conceived by a choreographer. This includes the moves, sequence of moves and patterns to be danced.

Counterpoint

Counterpoint is an expression of two opposing lines of material that form a contrasting balance. In music, a melodic line can be added below or above another line to create a unique theme. The word comes from the Latin *punctus contra punctum* which means *point against point*. In dance, this is often used to describe contrasting simultaneous movements.

Dynamics

The dynamics of something relates to its position in space and time including the manner in which a move is executed, from it flows energy and power. The execution, as well as space between these things, are often referred to as its dynamic. A dancer can vary these things to increase the impact and dynamics of movement and the dance.

Demi

Demi, from the French word for half is a ballet

definition that is used with another dance term. For example, demi-pointe.

Director

The director is often the choreographer but not always. A director will usually be in charge of production and the direction of elements including lighting and other performance staging elements. They are usually in charge of the direction of the piece and what the audience sees on stage. They often work in collaboration with others who help the director stage their vision.

Elevation

An elevated state is a raised state or action. It is also used to describe a jump or the ability to remain at the height (also known as the apex) of a jump or elevation.

Extension

An extension is a term used to describe the dancer's stretched out and raised leg. For example, during an arabesque, where your leg is extended behind your body.

Fouetté

A Fouetté is a quick whipping type movement when the leg is raised and often, but always, accompanied by a pirouette. However, the term fouetté is used to describe different types of ballet steps.

Flow

The word flow implies a continuous motion or sequence of moves or events and in dance often refers to momentum and the type and quality of movement.

Form

The simplest way to describe form in dance is to describe its shape. This is the way in which the movement occupies space and time.

Freestyle

Freestyle is improvisation or a free type of conceived dance, not necessarily constrained by pre-planned choreography. It is a spontaneous movement or a more spontaneous process than pre-planned choreography. Freestyle sections of choreography can sometimes be loosely planned but appear to be spontaneous. On the whole, however, they are made up on the spot.

Genre

Genre is the word which defines the classification of different styles of dance.

Gesture

A gesture is slightly different from a traditional dance move in the sense that it is a movement, but a lighter movement using your arms or legs to *suggest* or emphasise something. So, instead of moving your arms and hands to form a point, you could create a gesture which communicates the idea of a point without the full movement. It is a great way to communicate attitude and create a feeling in a subtle way.

Glissade

Glissade is a ballet term which means to glide and is used to describe the process of travelling, usually with linked jumps and is often itself, used as a linking move.

Grande

Grande is a ballet term which means large. It is used in conjunction with another term to describe the execution of a dance step often with the intention to make it bigger.

Grounded

To be grounded is to be connected to the floor and in dance is often used to describe the efficiency of the dancers' use of weight in connection with the floor.

Hold

A hold is when you literally hold a pose or a dance move from movement to stillness.

Improvisation

When you improvise you make something up as you go along, however within the dance world there are still sometimes rules in relation to improvisation depending on what genre or style of dance you are engaging in. That said, on the whole, an improvisation is completely improvised and created spontaneously by the dancer.

Isolation

Isolation describes the process of moving an isolated part of your body without moving the rest of your body.

Jeté

The term jeté used in conjunction with other steps and means dynamic movement, like a throw but especially a type of jump where the dancer extends a leg, jumps and then lands on the other leg.

Legato

Legato means smooth and connected in music and often conveys length usually with fluidity.

Line

Your line is the outline of your body, whilst you dance and perform.

Lunge

This is a movement where your weight is transferred forwards and onto your bent front leg.

It is sometimes called tombé which means fallen down.

Marking

To mark a piece means that you dance with less or minimal energy, focussing on timing, practising or learning rather than performing it with full energy. It is a way of conserving energy during rehearsals and also emphasising certain aspects of a piece at an energy rate less than that of full performance level.

Mirroring

This is when two dancers mirror each other by copying each other's movements as if one is standing in front of a mirror and the other dancer is your reflection, dancing with you.

Motif

This is usually the theme of a dance piece which can be delivered in dance by certain phrases or repetitive dance steps, gestures or movements.

Plié

A plié is a movement in which the dancer bends at the knees.

Pas

Pas is simply a term which means step.

Petit

Petit or Petite is usually used in conjunction with other steps and means small.

Pirouette

A pirouette is one of the most famous moves in ballet, which means to spin.

Phrase

A phrase is a section of choreography (often short).

Projection

Projection is the way in which you are communicating your movement and intention through the body in an expressive way. To project, in dance, often means to energetically communicate a movement.

Placement

Placement is where the dancer places their body including their legs and arms, for example. The placement is where it is located and can obviously be incorrect or correct.

Pointe Shoes

Pointe shoes are the shoes that ballet dancers wear to protect their toes. The shoes have a protective area so the dancer can safely dance on their toes. When a dancer does this it is called en pointe.

Sauté

Sauté means to jump and can be used alone or in conjunction with another step. A sauté arabesque, for example, would be an arabesque performed with a jump.

Stance

A stance is a posture that a dancer takes or holds.

Spotting

Spotting is a word which describes the placement of a dancer's head, whilst they turn. It's a technique which can help with controlling the turn and retaining control.

Sissonne

A Sissonne is a kind of jump from two to one foot creating a beautiful kind of scissor action visually before landing.

Snare

The snare is the sharp drum sound that is created by a drum with snares. It's that hard sound that you hear in a drum beat, like a clapping sound.

Tableau

A tableau is a frozen formation of dancers. It is a great way to open or close a dance performance and also a very impactful way to punctuate a piece of choreography if used in the right way.

Tempo

The tempo is the frequency and speed of a piece of music and is often described as a BPM (Beats Per Minute). Musically it is often measured with a metronome or in modern times with a click track by the drummer. However, when you learn a piece the choreographer can slow down the piece by changing the tempo.

Turnout

When the legs and feet are pointing in an outwards direction it is called turnout. This is created with outward rotation of the hips.

Unison

Unison is when a number of dancers dance the same movements at the same time. They dance uniformly and in unison.

Becoming a Good Dancer

Interestingly the basics of becoming a good dancer are the same basics you apply to become good in any field, which is essentially hard work and practice. There is no set path to become a good dancer, outside of practising, training and working hard. One of the main issues that I have come across with regards to dancer challenges is location and proximity to dance classes and dance schools which means that logistics and access to a dance education have a lot to do with the direction of careers. However, it's important that the dancer is empowered and understands that all options are available to them. It is for them to follow their own path and if need be, to build their own. The good dancer will do whatever it takes based on a number of factors and this could include moving to a city or applying for a dance school far away. There are many routes and directions you can go and there is no right or wrong way to make it as a good dancer.

It is important that you practise and become an expert in what you do. Practise your dance steps, choreography and freestyle. The enthusiastic dancer that will succeed does not need to be told this, it will come naturally. That natural drive translates into something else that you will need: confidence. Confidence breeds confidence and will make you attractive and inspire people. It's important that you are confident in yourself as a human being as well as a dancer. It's also important that you are friendly, presentable, clean and an easy person to work with. So attitude is very important when it comes to working as a dancer. Sometimes a dancer will lose a role because they are too hard to manage. This is much more frequent than you might think – a dancer won't get the role because they're an idiot, even if an incredible talent. Always remember this! Sometimes the less talented dancer can get the job because they are easier to work with and have a great attitude and energy.

Another important thing to try and develop is the direction of energy and life experience into your dance moves. I can say proudly, I put my whole life experience into every move I dance. Even when I rehearse, I put everything into it... I take each step very seriously. It's almost like each step is my last act or some kind of religious offering – never just "do the moves", dance like it is an honour and a privilege. This energy will project to the audience and even into the room during a dance class. Live the music and express it through your whole body. Don't forget your hands and face and eyes. Your facial expressions are extremely important too.

I 'lived' dance during my youth and beyond and in a sense I had no choice because I was performing on stage from before I was ten years old. However, if you live, like many of my students, in rural areas with fewer performance opportunities, I suggest that you do everything you can to create those opportunities for yourself. This might include entering dance competitions but might also involve waiting until you do have the chance to travel to a place where you have more dance classes and training opportunities. However, you must never just wait because you must, without excuse, use that time to train with what you do have. Read every dance book, learn from DVDs or online lessons, absorb from the greats through television. Connect with dancers and artists virtually and in the flesh. Learn about musicality… there is always, no matter where you are, opportunity to grow and expand as a dancer. Attend as many dance classes as you can and if you don't have any dance classes or you are beyond the local standard then take advantage of this and create a dance class. You could do this with friends or create something for children or other budding dancers – don't be afraid to create a dance path for yourself. The same lessons that you will learn will give you experience that you will utilise as you grow as a performer and a dancer.

It's also important to balance your schedule because dancing is a physical activity and you will feel tired at times. It's also important to remember that to become the best dancer that you can be, you should be able to express different aspects of life, which means that you should experience as much of life as you can. That means that you should study history and literature and the arts in general, not only because this is a wonderful intelligent thing to do but because it will, without question, help you become a more effective communicator and dancer. It will also help you decide whether dance is what you really want to do. I suggest you keep your options open and really think about the direction of your life because no matter what happens, you will do what you end up doing anyway, so there is nothing to lose.

Dancing is something that you should enjoy and do naturally and it should be fun. If it's fun for you, then working hard will be having fun and you will succeed. Keeping an open mind will also help you keep your artistic mind expanding and this includes dance style. Make sure that you try as many different styles as you can; identify what you like and gain experience. You can use that experience and maybe later learn to fuse dance styles or moves. Once you've tried various styles you will naturally lean towards one or the other. These can be your foundation dance styles that you can focus on with your basic ballet technique. It's not necessarily that every dancer has a foundation in ballet but it is certainly strongly suggested and encouraged because your options and opportunities will be restricted if you don't have a basic solid ballet foundation.

Don't be afraid to dance for yourself. This is when you find an empty dance studio or dance in your bedroom. Express your physicality, play the music, practise and have fun. You will be shocked at how many times your creativity will flow and things will happen. Often your creativity will be more likely to flow in this type of environment than any type of official or formal dance class or setting.

John's Story: Facing your Fears

If you have read my *Performers Book* you will already have heard the story of John but I think it's such an inspirational story it's worth me telling it again – here – especially as John's story directly relates to his personal fear of dance and it exemplifies the old adage that it's never too late to start. Often succeeding in the dance world will be directly linked to your ability to motivate yourself, believe in yourself and to overcome your fears. We all have fears and we all have the ability to overcome them. Our artistic prime is beyond those fears. Let's take a closer look…

John Dover, a successful businessman, owner of one of the top chains of bakeries in London, which he built from nothing – was fed up. Although he was a successful businessman who, on the surface, looked like he had everything, there was just one thing that always bugged him. He was afraid of dancing and felt he couldn't do it. This had a major impact on the quality of his social interactions and he hadn't danced for years. Whenever he went to weddings or found the courage to go into a club, he would just stand at the side and have a drink. The problem for John was that this had gone on for so long it was really getting to him. When he could bear it no longer, he reached the point where the unhappiness outweighed the fear of seeking help. Although in his mind, it was impossible for him to dance or be taught, he plucked up the courage to go to the dance school's website and make contact. This might have caused embarrassment but for him it was a big step. And no more embarrassing than all those years of standing on the side-lines.

I asked him to tell me what he wanted me to do for him and what he wanted to get out of this, what were his aims? He was convinced there was no hope but there was a big wedding coming up, and it would be nice not to go straight to the bar when the music started. He went on to say that he was kind of large and shy as well. Interesting. The great thing is that he was totally honest and upfront from the beginning. He had nothing to lose and everything to gain. No ego and no expectations... We arranged to meet at the dance studios. John later went on to describe his fear when he entered the building and how it made him feel intimidated. Well as I saw him across the canteen above the studio, I thought to myself, "This guy looks great and very established." He explained how he felt and I told him not to worry. After we got started, I asked him to show me how he usually dances. He told me that he doesn't at all, and hasn't ever.

Interesting – but not a barrier.

The curious thing is that because he had nothing to lose and everything to gain, he just listened and repeated and repeated (and repeated!) until he started to get it. After a few private lessons he said that he now had the courage to try a public dance class. He came prepared, early and ready to go. He hid in the corner and tried his hardest, but he survived and met lots of like-minded people. It's a different world on the other side of the glass and everyone is in the same boat trying to learn. Now John started to come more and more regularly; within two to three months he had moved up to the front of the class and people were asking him how long he had been attending. John thought this was unbelievable! He was just a baker who couldn't dance. But he was progressing because he took action; he took that first impossible step. But that's not the end of the story.

John came out for a drink with some friends, one of which was a casting director who was looking for one more male who could act, for a commercial. He said that John looked perfect for the job and could he come along to the casting? Now you have to remember that this is all a big joke to John… MD of a big company, being asked to be in commercials… this was all too surreal! Well, within a few weeks John was on television in a music commercial. After that, he was contacted by one of the biggest dairy companies in the world who thought that he would make a perfect baker in their commercial too… big money and worldwide!

John's life had transformed in a matter of weeks and his confidence was soaring. He had learned to let go of his fear and to just relax. He had learned to dance and he had made lots of new friends along the way and now was on his way to becoming a star too! Wow! The transformation from that first email to now is shocking. But the most important thing in John's story is that he took the first fearful step and then he just proceeded to take more little steps. Just small steps, nothing immediately life-changing or earth shattering and look at the positive transformation.

He is exactly the same person who wrote that first email, just with a different attitude and perspective.

Oh, and one more thing…the wedding!

John travels off to his best friend's wedding and boy did he have a surprise lined up. During the dancing, the announcement came over the loudspeakers to clear the dance floor… John was going to do a dance solo. He was going to perform. The music came on, he did it, the whole place erupted in applause. He had won, he had overcome another challenge that he thought was impossible and not only had he overcome it, but he also obliterated all self-doubt. But there's more… at the wedding he meets a girl who thinks that he's amazing and is impressed by his dancing skills. She moves over to London and they're now getting married! Now that's a great story. John is an amazing man and I am honoured to be part of somebody's dreams coming true.

Take the small step. You have nothing to lose. Take a look at the character Edmond Dantes in

Alexandre Dumas' *The Count of Monte Cristo*. For the first couple of years of his imprisonment in the Château d'If, he sat banging his head against the solid rock wall doing nothing but turning to madness and then after a long period of time he realised something. He started scratching at the wall, and small fragments would fall off, admittedly they were almost invisible, but after a few hours, he had scraped off about a handful. He calculated that if he had done this for two years, instead of squandering his time, then he could have dug a passage two feet across and twenty feet deep. And realising this, the prisoner regretted not having devoted the long hours that had already passed, ever so slowly, to the task... however slow the work, how much would he have achieved in the six or so years that he had spent buried in this dungeon! The idea fired him with renewed enthusiasm. The message is clear: **the time you spend procrastinating – could be time doing!** Take hope from Edmond Dante (and John!). Edmond escaped the terrible dungeon of the Château d'If by slow, seemingly tedious fruitless digging through solid rock... but over time it worked for him and he achieved his goal. All you need is time and a small amount of action toward your desired goal and you'll be on the right track.

Facing Your Fears

YouTuber Rob Robinson737 wrote the following extremely insightful comment underneath Massive Attack's 'Angel' video, about three years ago:

"The video is about running away from your fears, the longer you run away from them the greater they become until you reach a point from where you can no longer run as if there is no land left for you to run on and there it is your greatest fears stood there right in front of you, and then you realise that these fears are just an illusion and that you confront them head-on and then they are frightened of you at the moment you start chasing them."

The video has almost 30,000,000 views and I encourage you to go and watch it. Massive Attack's 'Angel' is from their *Mezzanine* album, released in 1998. The English trip hop group didn't actually release their video at the time as told by **massiveattack.ie;**

"At the time of the single release of Angel, Massive Attack decided (for cited reasons as not capturing the mood of the song) to not use the already shot promo video for Angel (which had reputably cost £20,000 to

shoot) to promote the single. For this reason, the video would remain unseen for over three years where it would finally see the light of day on the Eleven Promos DVD release."

The video really captures, visually, the tragedy of not facing our fears head-on. We have a choice and once we face them, we realise that we are only running away from ourselves anyway. This process is actually called 'exposure'. This exposure to your fears gradually can help you build a kind of resistance and lower anxiety until you can overcome said fear. Never be afraid of exposure. The great teacher Napoleon Hill said, "Fears are nothing more than a state of mind" and he was right. In fact, when you feel or can sense potential 'exposure' that is often the first place you should 'go' to grow and evolve. This is really expressed perfectly in 'Angel'. With regard to fear, I actually mean unfounded fear. Or the fear of fear.

For example, some fight or flight responses are perfectly reasonable and I am not talking about that kind of normal life-saving fear… I am talking about the different type of fear, the illegitimate one that is the fear of fear itself that we run away from often in our lives. That is what needs to be faced directly to advance creatively and it is expressed extremely well by Massive Attack.

Remember the words of the great Henry Ford:

"One of the greatest discoveries a man makes, one of his great surprises, is to find he can do what he was afraid he couldn't do."

Other Tips

- If you need to seek professional help, absolutely do so!
- If you need some help from a trusted friend feel free to ask for it.
- Own your fears and face them head-on. They are part of your current personality.
- Write down your fears and evaluate the risk level and logically analyse the potential consequences of taking the risk.
- Reward yourself if you attempt to overcome it.
- If you fail, do not blame yourself. Keep working at it because practice makes perfect and every time you fail you gain experience and are one step closer to resolution.

Scientific Reasons to Face your Fears Head-on

Paul W. Frankland and Sheena A. Josselyn wrote an article in *Science* magazine called *Facing your Fears* (a PERSPECTIVE NEUROSCIENCE article – Science 15 Jun 2018: Vol. 360, Issue 6394, pp. 1186-1187 DOI: 10.1126/science.aau0035) and they stated something very interesting;

"… treating no-longer-threatening situations as dangerous may be maladaptive and lead to anxiety disorders, including phobias and post-traumatic stress disorder. Central to many forms of therapy designed to tackle these anxiety disorders is the idea that to overcome fear, one needs to face it."

Maladaptive is defined as "not adjusting adequately or appropriately to the environment or situation". So this means that scientifically speaking, facing your fears is the healthy thing to do because if you don't it, can lead to, as they clearly state, "anxiety disorders, including phobias and post-traumatic stress disorder". So, not only is it the logical thing to do, but it is also healthy for you… and most often, easier than you suspect.

Your Creative Prime is on the Other Side of your Fear

This is why an artist has to constantly push their internal and external boundaries to expand creatively. This is all part of the creative journey and nothing to worry about because it's a never-ending expansion. Every artist will have some kind of fear before they pass it and extend outside of their comfort zone. Once they reach their destination, it begins again… that's just the way it is! It's the same for us all. Once you understand this then the fear of fear fades. That means your greatest painting, greatest composition or greatest work is just one step outside of your comfort zone, through the fear zone… it's right there if you want it.

The Psychology of Auditions

I'm going to give two seemingly opposing pieces of advice. Both are valid according to context. That might sound paradoxical but that's life. Auditions are part of a dancer's life. Getting through them – and with success – has as much to do with your psychology as your talent. Auditions and castings are the main route to jobs and work in the dance and entertainment world, however it's important to point out… they are not the only route.

I actually believe that *some* people should never audition for anything, because the process will restrict their growth as a dancer. However, I suspect that these people are a rarity. If I had to put an estimate on the number, I'd suggest that one in twenty people should not submit to an audition process because it will be restrictive, a waste of time, energy and not conducive to success. With that said I suggest that 95% of people, if they feel the need to audition, should do so and do so as effectively and enthusiastically as possible.

Statistically speaking, with regards to auditions specifically, you have a high probability of failure, so what is there to lose? If you read the paragraph above and were triggered then I suggest that you are not the type of person who should even consider a route, other than the traditional i.e. auditioning, casting or submitting to someone else's decision. However, if you are the type of person who does not submit and feels that the process will be too demeaning, no matter what the benefit then, I have a great suggestion just for you.

Create projects for yourself and give yourself the starring role!

Not everybody is designed to do this, but it's easier now than ever before. You have a platform with social media and the tools and technology readily available. You could even film a movie or a dance video. Although I can't offer any scientific data to back this up, only gut feeling based on experience, I am pretty sure that if you are the type of person with the drive to create a project and push to its conclusion, then you will probably be able to push with a much higher probability of success than a simple audition. In an audition what you have to remember is nearly every factor and variable to determine your success is out of your control. I guarantee that you will learn more, grow and also enjoy the experience. You will at least enjoy the experience more than the 95% –99.9% of people who are rejected.

The Probability of Audition Success

I typed in to Google 'audition to booking ratio' and I am pleased to see that it correlates with my approximate observation of the industry, at best: 5% (or a one in twenty chance of audition success). **backstage.com** in a 2010 article entitled *Booking Ratios* by 'secret agent man' state:

"A booking ratio is exactly what it sounds like: two numbers that represent how many jobs you've booked compared to how many auditions you've had. So if your ratio is one out of 20, that means it took 20 auditions for you to land one job".

However, I would suggest that this is probably the average best case scenario because the author points out, in the same article:

"One of my most promising young clients has been out on something like 40 auditions and hasn't booked a single job."

In reality, people can audition much more than that and get 100% rejection. Cecilia Capuzzi Simon's *New York Times* April 2008 article "Try-outs for the Rest of Your Life" describes:

"all told, a record 1,200 students were auditioning for 16 spots in the fall acting class or 12 in the musical theatre program."

That's approximately closer to a 98% failure rate. I have seen successful people crushed psychologically because of repeated failed auditions. On the other hand, I have friends who got an audition and became some of the most famous people in the world. I suggest that you do take action that is conducive to your own mental wellbeing and corresponds with your own realistic chances of success. That means, that you may have an amazing record of success with auditioning and casting and maybe you enjoy it … you should continue. However, I suggest that if this is not the case then you should invest in yourself and create your own projects because then at least you are in control of the outcome and ultimately you can control its success and impact in the world. However, there are relatively few people who will do the work required. Relatively few people who have the drive to travel down that road. Possibly less than 5%, which means that it's probably the same success rate as auditioning anyway, with the exception that you are almost 100% in control of whether you succeed or not, compared to almost 0% control when somebody else is making the decisions. With that said, only you know what is the best route for you. Here are some audition tips to increase your chances and also improve your psychological wellbeing before, during and after an audition.

Beware!

An audition is not a natural healthy environment. It can leave you feeling drained, dehumanised and often rejected. Statistically, you will almost certainly be rejected with very little feedback. Although this is normal in the entertainment industry, this is not a normal in any other realms of life. It is completely reasonable to be upset by this or have a negative psychological reaction. However, it's best to know this in advance and take remedial action. There are obviously different types of auditions depending on your craft. Here are some quick general tips and pointers.

Audition tips and advice

- Get an agent! This will make your life easier and increase your chances of success.
- Read the audition instructions carefully in advance and follow the notice carefully.
- Good preparation is key.
- Always bring an up to date photo/picture and CV/resume.
- Always be professional and don't make excuses under any circumstances.
- Be consistent and resilient. If you choose to audition, go all the way and all in!
- Remember that your first impression is key. Walk in with confidence, good posture and smile.
- Keep your energy up until you leave the building/area, not just the room. You might still might bump into somebody important on your way out!
- Dress appropriately and if this is not stated, dress smart casual.
- Pick material that is personally linked to you, something that you are passionate

about.

- Psyche yourself up and make sure that you prepare your energy levels so that you are ready.
- Make eye contact and don't worry. This is meaningless in the grand scheme of the universe anyway!
- Once it's over, let it go and refocus on the next one. Don't think about it again unless to analyse and actively work on improving your technique.

Motivation and Drive

What motivates you to perform, dance or create? This is such a pertinent question because it's essentially the foundation of what you do and will direct your artistic endeavours and in actual fact, your whole life. At the very least, this should ideally be conscious, rather than unconscious. Consequently, the question of whether your drives are an actual choice or compulsion is very important. Could your drive to succeed in any sphere of the arts or sports actually be a way of solving unresolved childhood or psychological issues? Could you be attempting to resolve them directly by performing or creating? Are you addicted to that process and could you let it go if you chose to?

It's important to really understand your motivations and the root cause of your drives because they may well not be positive for you. In other words, you might feel resolution by performing but in actual fact realise, later, that it didn't solve your issues and that you were actually running away from fears or from root issues in your life. Many pop stars have talked about becoming a musician to get girls. This is absolutely the case and not just a flippant remark. It's often as simple as this when we look at our true motivations. I would suggest that no matter what your true motivations are... let them be conscious and at the very least, understand them.

Once you've identified your drives ... are you doing it right?

'Never give up' is a popular saying but it's crazy if you think about it. If you are doing things correctly and the way they need to be done to work and conducive to success, then continue. However, if things are not working then you should at the very least, give up on what you are doing and change course or change your actions and behaviours. If you have tried this multiple times for an amount of time (that only you can determine) and still 'fail', then logic alone will tell you that it's not for you and that you should give up and try something else. Or a different way of putting it is to give up doing something the wrong way and start doing it the right way. Things can only work if you are doing them the right way. It's important to be honest with yourself and also to accept your own limitations and that things are not in your control. Not everything will happen the way you want them to happen... and that is fine. That is what makes life magical! The most important thing is that you ask *yourself* the question and don't listen to other people's opinions on what *you* should be doing because they don't know what your inner drives and motivations are. You owe it to yourself to know as this will help you succeed and live your life to its maximum and achieve your potential in a healthy way.

How do you know when I should change the course or give up?

Only you know the answer to this question. Writer Anthony Cerullo, in his article 'Why Science Says It's Okay to Give Up on Your Music Career Goals' from the sonicbids blog, makes a great point:

"One quick and easy way to judge this is with stress. If you're feeling so stressed about a particular goal that it has a negative effect on your life, then perhaps it's time to drop it. Goals are supposed to be challenging,

but you shouldn't need sleeping pills to fall asleep or be in a state of depression just to achieve them."

I agree with Anthony Cerullo completely.

Never give up... the real deal

There are some people, who do things the right way and have the drive and ability to succeed at their given task or artistic goal. As long as they are fulfilled and happy then they should never give up. It's as simple as that because it is that individual who will certainly succeed. Whether you are that person or not is a determination that only you can make. Either way, if you are right or wrong, it probably won't have any impact on the probability of success anyway, so it's important that you be honest with yourself so that you can put your energy and life force into something that will actually fulfil you and works for you.

Dance Education:
Private Lessons or Public Classes?

Without a doubt, one of the questions which I get asked most is "Should I take public classes or private lessons?" and I always answer it the same way, "Don't waste your money on expensive private lessons!" However, there is a caveat – unless you are very rich and have money to burn or, most importantly, you have something specific or specialised that you want to learn for an event or something in particular.

The reason for this is because if you are a beginner or near the beginning of your career you really just need to get going and build an experience based on the basics. This is exactly what you will get in an open dance class. Another thing which you gain is the experience of dancing in a group with no pressure. Even though you might think that there is pressure on you in an open public dance class, the truth is, that people focus on themselves and if you stand to the side and focus on the teacher and what you are learning calmly and without drawing attention to yourself, you will probably be ignored and left to focus on your lesson. People really are too busy looking in the mirror and worrying about themselves to worry about you, so you have nothing to worry about! So in a way, you lose that pressure of the focus being on you, you can almost be absorbed in the class and over time you will gain expertise and experience. Your skills and dance reasoning skills may actually increase at a faster rate than private lessons because the instructions won't necessarily be catered uniquely to you alone, which means that you will have to be quick in picking things up. That skill comes very quickly in group classes and I mean within three to five lessons you will find that your retaining skills are exponentially higher than when you first started as a beginner.

If somebody has a specific thing they want to learn or train for then that is fine for private lessons and choreography. However, I like to suggest a mix of open and private classes because then you gain both skills from both experiences. Obviously, in a private lesson, I can cater it exactly to your needs and hyper-focus on correction or whatever you may need. However, often what is needed is not even physiological, it is psychological – and that confidence can sometimes be earned in an open forum rather than privately. There are other times when schedule or even times when VIPs cannot entertain the idea of attending a public open class. This is often the case with royalty, however, I have found that even the most famous actors and actresses can attend a dance class and blend in unnoticed.

In summary, if you want to learn a general style I would suggest open public classes. If you have something specialised or specific to train for, then I would suggest private sessions. Ideally, you should be able to learn in almost any situation or environment including via DVD or online because it's just a case of following instructions and listening.

Dance Injuries

All dancers will get an injury at one time or other. It may be mild or it may be severe but it's a natural part of a dancer's life. With that said, ideally, this can be kept to a minimum with some thought, looking after yourself and your body and good preparation. It goes without saying that dance is a physical activity and it is physically demanding with hours of repetition. If you dance for five hours a day, no matter who you are, it will have an impact on your body and you will feel fatigued at times and over time your risk of stress fractures or other injuries will increase. The good news is that there are so many things that you can do to prevent this and to keep the risk to a minimum.

I don't actually believe that a dancer in training particularly needs to do much else as regards to exercise, like going to the gym, for example, although building core strength isn't a bad thing. Many hours of dance training and practice per day will certainly keep you strong, flexible your stamina levels high. However, keeping your body strong and fit will help you become less susceptible to injury, as will keeping yourself healthy. With that said, one of the main dance injuries is a sprained ankle which is obviously due to impact. Another word for that impact is trauma and trauma injuries are not unusual in dancers. It's important to remember that if you tear a ligament, for example, that you build strength because they don't heal to their pre-injury strength and the risk of recurrence increases, so one must also be more vigilant. However, that vigilance can sometimes make a dancer even more injury prone due to lack of focus. This is why strong technique and preparation are key. This includes an appropriate warm-up and an appropriate cool down. Give yourself ample time for this because it is an investment in your body and will give you longevity.

Other tips include:

- Make sure that you are hydrated during class.
- Make sure that you have eaten and are nourished.
- Make sure that you get enough sleep before class and are appropriately rested.

- Build up your core strength with cross training or in the gym if need be.
- Make sure you dress appropriately and especially wear the correct properly fitting shoes.
- Act appropriately and healthily.
- If you injured seek professional medical advice immediately.

With regards to rest, the truth is that it is up to your body how much rest you need. Make sure you listen to your body and watch your mood because it will indicate to you when you are rested or not. I also suggest running a few times a week to keep your cardio levels up. I personally increase my runs when leading up to and preparing for a performance to make sure that I can run at a fast pace, at the very least, for the equivalent amount of time I will be performing on stage.

Now, it's important to know the difference between discomfort and pain. You will experience discomfort when engaging in the activity of dance but if you feel a pain that keeps you awake or that pain exists before you start dancing and persists or worsens then you should immediately seek medical attention from a doctor or physiotherapist.

The International Association for Dance Medicine & Science advice

The International Association for Dance Medicine & Science (www.iadms.org) have a great resource page, written by Nadia Sefcovic, DPT, COMT and Brenda Critchfield, MS, ATC under the auspices of the Education Committee of IADMS which explains the "Price" acronym which is important for you to learn because, as they state; "using PRICED as a first aid method immediately after an injury helps limit the inflammation and the pain and can also guide continuing care and rehabilitation":

PROTECTION: Remove additional danger or risk from the injured area
REST: Stop dancing and stop moving the injured area
ICE: Apply ice to the injured area for 20 minutes every two hours
COMPRESSION: Apply an elastic compression bandage to the injured area
ELEVATION: Raise the injured area above the heart
DIAGNOSIS: Acute injuries should be evaluated by a health-care professional

The International Association for Dance Medicine & Science also use the "Harm" acronym which they point out should be avoided in the days soon after an injury:

HEAT: Any kind of heat will speed up the circulation, resulting in more swelling and a longer recovery
ALCOHOL: Alcohol can increase swelling, causing a longer recovery
RUNNING OR OTHER EXCESSIVE EXERCISE: Exercising too early can cause further damage to the injured part. Exercise also increases blood flow, resulting in more swelling
MASSAGE: Massage increases swelling and bleeding into the tissue, prolonging recovery time

I strongly suggest you familiarise yourself with their website and always remember to consult your doctor if in any doubt whatsoever.

Some of the Greatest Dancers and Choreographers of All Time

You can learn a great deal by looking at the greats. Here is a partial list of some of the greatest dancers and choreographers of all time who have made an impact in the world of dance and entertainment

Fred Astaire

Fred Astaire was born on May 10th 1899 in Omaha, Nebraska, USA and died on June 22nd 1987. In my opinion, he was the greatest dancer of all time and is certainly one of the most influential. He starred in thirty-one musical films and at least ten stage musicals (in London and on Broadway), including numerous TV specials. Fred Astaire was a virtuoso dancer who revolutionised dance on film. This included dancing on the ceiling and walls in 'You're All the World to Me' from *Royal Wedding* (1951). Talking about his process he said:

"Working out the steps is a very complicated process—something like writing music. You have to think of some step that flows into the next one, and the whole dance must have an integrated pattern. If the dance is right, there shouldn't be a single superfluous movement. It should build to a climax and stop!"

From *Astaire Dancing – The Musical Films* by John Mueller (1986 – Alfred A. Knopf).

Gene Kelly is another Hollywood giant and star of dance and film and he said that 'the history of dance on film begins with Astaire.' Choreographer, Jerome Robbins, would go on to say, 'Astaire's dancing looks so simple, so disarming, so easy, yet the understructure, the way he sets the steps on, over or against the music, is so surprising and inventive.' Fred Astaire was known for being a perfectionist and my favourite dance performance of his is 'Puttin on the Ritz' from *Blue Skies* (1946) and various scenes from *Funny Face* (1957), including the 'Mac scene'. I also strongly advise that you watch the complete *That's Entertainment!* (1974) series of films to learn about the dance in Hollywood and the greats.

Gene Kelly

Gene Kelly was born in Pittsburgh, Pennsylvania, the USA on August 23rd 1912 and died at the age of eighty-three on February 2nd 1996. He was a Hollywood giant and known for his athletic dance style. He is most well known for his incredible dance performance in *Singin' in the Rain* (1952). He revolutionised Hollywood dance and is credited with introducing ballet to the masses via motion picture. In 1945 he choreographed and danced in a ground-breaking film called *Anchors Aweigh* which was a live-action performance with the cartoon mouse, Jerry Mouse, which gave him, renewed critical acclaim.

The Nicholas Brothers

The Nicholas Brothers were a dance team of brothers called Fayard (1914–2006) and Harold (1921–2000). They danced a style called 'flash dance' which combined tap dancing with acrobatics. It was very prominent in the 1920s and 1930s. 'Jumpin Jive' performed by Cab Calloway and the Nicholas Brothers from *Stormy Weather* (1943) is one of the best dance performances on film of all time. It is incredible! Please take careful note of the next sentence: Fayard and Harold had no formal dance training! They learned by watching and imitating professional dancers from the Vaudeville shows and other performances. They would even go on to teach tap master classes at Harvard University.

"My brother (Harold) and I used our whole bodies, our hands, our personalities and everything."

Fayard Nicholas interview USA Today (2005) – Published 1/25/2006

The same interview had a quote from Fred Astaire who said:

"Astaire once told the brothers that the acrobatic elegance and synchronicity of the Jumpin' Jive dance sequence in Stormy Weather (1943) made it the greatest movie musical number he had ever seen."

Mikhail Baryshnikov

Mikhail Baryshnikov was born in Latvia (the former Soviet Union) on January 27th 1948. He is simply one of the greatest male ballet dancers of all time and my favourite performance is Albrechts' variation from act II of the romantic ballet, *Giselle* (1977). He floats with grace and performs with incredible strength and power. He defected from the Soviet Union to Canada in 1974. The *New York Times* critic, Clive Barnes said that he was 'the most perfect dancer I have ever seen.'

John Travolta

John Travolta was born on February 18th 1954 in Englewood, New Jersey, USA and in my opinion, is one of the most underrated dancers of all time. He is well known for his musical roles in *Saturday Night Fever* (1977) and *Grease* (1978) as well as some of the biggest movies of all time. His disco dance moves influenced other greats of dance in the 1970s and 1980s. He taught Michael Jackson, who incorporated many of his moves into his music videos and performances including, 'Smooth Criminal'. Travolta famously danced with Diana, Princess of Wales, at the White House on November 9th 1985 and the black dress she wore went on to be known as the 'Travolta dress'. It was auctioned and became the most expensive dress at around £250,000 in 2013.

Bob Fosse

Bob Fosse, choreographer and filmmaker, was born in Chicago, Illinois, the USA on June 23rd 1927 and died on September 23rd 1987. He directed and choreographed the great musicals, *Chicago* in 1975 and *Cabaret* in 1972. He created a distinct style of choreography and is linked with the term 'jazz hands' for his prominent use of hands and lines. He choreographed and directed the film *Sweet Charity* in 1969 which starred Shirley MacLaine from the original Broadway musical (which he originally directed and choreographed). He is well known for his use of hats and gloves and he choreographed one of the most spectacular dance performances on film, from *Sweet Charity* called the 'Rich Man's Frug'. He was surely one of the greats and a real innovator.

Wade Robson

Wade Robson is one of the greatest dancers and choreographers of all time. He is also a world-changing advocate of child welfare and a great teacher. He was born on September 17th 1982 in Brisbane, Australia. He choreographed some of their most iconic choreography of the 2000s including artists such as NSYNC and Britney Spears. His choreography for the NSYNC song 'No Strings Attached' is one of the great pieces of pop choreography, in my opinion. He hosted his own MTV dance show called *The Wade Robson Project* and judged US show *So You Think You Can Dance*. Wade Robson was known to study animals and include their movements into his choreography, even when he was a young man. He is one of the greatest pop choreographers and dancers of all time and you can find out more about him on his website: **www.waderobson.com**

Michael Flatley

Michael Flatley is an American Irish dancer born on July 16th 1958 Chicago, Illinois, USA. He is most well known for *Riverdance* and *Lord of the Dance*. Flatley 'reinvented' Irish dance and brought it to worldwide acclaim. He is one of the most famous and richest dancers in the world.

Rudolf Nureyev

Rudolf Nureyev is widely known as one of the best ballet dancers of all time. He was born in Russia on March 17th 1938 and died in France on January

6th 1993. He defected to the west in 1961, even though the KGB were monitoring him and tried to stop him. He went on to serve as chief choreographer and director of the Paris Opera Ballet.

Josephine Baker

Josephine Baker was an iconic dancer born on 3rd June 1906, St. Louis, Missouri, USA and died on the 12th April 1975 in Paris, France, where her career was mainly based. She became the most famous dancer of Folies Bergère in Paris, known worldwide. Her image was iconic and her costumes even included artificial bananas! She became a visual symbol of the art deco and jazz age in the 1920s with her striking look and erotic performances. Writer Ernest Hemingway, according to her website, is said to have called her "the most sensational woman anyone ever saw". Josephine Baker is probably most well known for dancing the Charleston and swing but the truth is that she had her own unique style. She also, in addition to being an amazing performer, was an amazing human being contributing to the Civil Rights Movement by refusing to perform to segregated audiences and even being awarded the

Chevalier of the Légion d'honneur by General Charles de Gaulle for aiding the resistance during World War Two.

Part 2

Health, Fitness and Nutrition

You Are What You Eat

"Dieting is no substitute for exercise" – Dr Mileham Hayes

You'd think that dancers would be the healthiest people out there ... you'd be wrong! Many dancers will chomp down a banana between classes rather than eat a meal, skip breakfast. Too many dancers smoke and drink excessive amounts of alcohol. Appearances can be misleading. So, let's take a look at the basics...

The foundation of a healthy lifestyle is diet and exercise. The two have a symbiotic relationship and both are keys to a dancer's wellbeing. It's also important to realise that diet is no substitute for exercise. You can eat a healthy balanced diet and still be unfit and perform well below your optimum without exercise, and you will perform well below your optimum level if you exercise regularly but have a poor unhealthy diet. You need to have both:

a healthy balance and you will see amazing results in your dancing, fitness, lifestyle and general wellbeing.

We process food at different rates, as we all have a unique metabolism. But it is quite clear that there is no magic formula or secret diet that will work for all… because we are all different, but it is possible to find a metabolic balance, where you nourish yourself to your optimum level whilst consuming the right healthy amounts of fats, which leads to a healthy balance, your wellbeing and your ideal body weight. One thing is quite clear; healthy, logical moderation is key… quick fix diets and popular fads are temporary solutions that can damage your long term health and are not solid foundations for a healthy lifestyle. If you become aware of how you eat and the different reasons why, including any psychological attachments that you may have to certain foods, then you can become more in tune with your body and its needs and change your lifestyle and improve the quality of your life.

Some Basic Advice

Let's face it, we're all pretty busy and don't have the time to be keeping a daily food diary and counting every calorie that we consume with every mouthful wherever we may be. And the good news is that it's just totally unnecessary! If you focus on eating within a natural framework and only eat when you are hungry and stop when you are comfortably full, you will begin to retrain your mind and body and retain your natural body weight in a healthy sustained way. Crazy diets and quick fixes are not necessary.

A Simple Healthy Framework

What is a healthy framework? Well, a healthy framework is simply three healthy meals a day. And if you are hungry, two healthy snacks daily as well. This is your foundation and a solid daily framework that will give you all that you need to function healthily and to your optimum level as well as attain and maintain healthy body weight. It generally makes sense to have a fairly substantial meal, as early as possible in the day to give you energy and to give you a kick start and keep you going with a healthy sustained energy release throughout the morning. But it is also important to remember that you eat, within the framework, when you feel comfortable and it may not be feasible due to time restraints or other everyday factors, to have a very large breakfast first thing in the morning and would rather have a larger meal later in the day. This is absolutely fine, as it is your body and different strategies work for different types of people. You need to find out what works best for you and what makes you comfortable within the natural healthy framework.

Before we take a closer look at the various types of healthy macronutrients that the body needs to function healthily I should add one more important thing. Metabolic balance and healthy food intake will help you focus naturally on the right foods for you and increase the level of your wellbeing. After you have felt and observed the effect of positive dietary change you will not feel the urge to eat unhealthily and give up your energy and wellbeing because of some temporary cravings that only give you short term pleasure and a quick high (and can leave you feeling dejected afterwards). They are usually physiological level issues and will be addressed when you start to maintain a healthy balanced diet, naturally. Until that point it is important to keep sight of your goal and if you are overweight or unhappy with your lifestyle, to follow the most simple advice in the book. This might sound crazy, but if you follow this simple advice you will accelerate toward your goals: stop eating foods that you know make you fat, quick fix snacks that give you short term pleasure at the expense of your long term wellbeing.

Yes, it's that simple, and it's a decision for you to make when you feel comfortable enough to do it. I guarantee you that, you cannot fail if you stick to a healthy balanced diet, but the choice is yours. You cannot fail if you simply eat the right foods for your body and overcome the urges, bad habits and food cravings that you know are detrimental to your mental and physical wellbeing. Why not take a look at it from a different psychological level. If you had diabetes or heart disease, you would be advised by your doctor to stop eating certain foods, and the probability is that you would do it so that you can enjoy life. I say that you, right now, have the chance to preserve your life and wellbeing and really live life to the maximum by changing your outlook and diet and becoming a better version of who you are today. And that means that you may want to take an honest look at your fat intake and those unhealthy foods that you know are detrimental to your health and cut them out. Just do it! Keep sight of your longer-term goals and you'll be amazed at how it will get easier and easier, once you get going…the key is to get going! Let's take a closer look at healthy eating and what the body needs, namely, carbohydrates, proteins and fats.

Carbohydrates

Simple and Complex Carbohydrates

There are two major types of carbohydrates in foods: simple and complex.

Simple carbohydrates (also known as simple sugars) include glucose, lactose, sucrose, fructose and galactose, which are found in the sugar that we use in our tea, honey, some fruits as well as in milk and dairy products. Obviously, fruit and milk products are a lot better to consume compared to pure sugar and sweets because they contain other important nutrients like calcium, fibre and other vitamins. As opposed to pure refined sugar, in fizzy drinks for example, which might give you a quick short term burst of energy (and no other nutrients), but will go straight to your cells to be stored… and not invisibly or without consequences, I hasten to add.

Complex carbohydrates, on the other hand, are starches and contain nutrients, complicated sugars as well as fibre. Complex carbohydrates serve as a much more efficient and healthy fuel for the body and the nutrients and fibre when broken down by the body, are stored and can easily be converted into energy, for when it is needed, in a slow release efficient way.

Another type of carbohydrate, found in foods which have lost their goodness, vitamins and minerals, due to refinement, are called 'refined complex carbohydrates'. They have had their skins and fibres removed and consequently, behave in the same way as simple carbohydrates, causing insulin production to increase and can be found in white flour, white rice and other refined foods that have lost that natural goodness. Additionally, white bread and other refined carbohydrates are usually combined with hydrogenated fats and pure sugar to improve the taste... not so good!

Complex Carbohydrates

Include: *whole grains, whole wheat pasta (i.e. brown), brown bread, brown rice, muesli, potatoes, cauliflower, tomatoes, onions, kidney beans, carrots, cabbage, lentils, broccoli.*

Simple Carbohydrates

Include: *white bread, sugar, white pasta, cakes, fizzy drinks, fruit juices, chocolate, jams, most processed cereals, alcoholic drinks and all products made with white flour.*

Consumption of these types of carbohydrate causes your blood sugar level to rise at drastically different rates. And it is important that your blood sugar level is regulated, guarding against heart disease and diabetes, for example. When you consume simple carbohydrates, it effectively raises your hormone insulin stimulation very quickly, whose job it is to regulate and keep the sugar level at a normal healthy level. This is because simple carbohydrates are absorbed very quickly into the bloodstream, quickly raising the blood sugar level. Complex (unrefined) carbohydrates, on the other hand, release sugar into the bloodstream at a sustained slow rate over a much longer period. They are also rich in fibre. The key is sustained healthy consumption and the release of its goodness over time as opposed to a quick fix, that doesn't last and is detrimental to your health.

Fibre

Fibre is found in unrefined grains and complex carbohydrates. It helps your digestive system work well, which is integral to your feeling of wellbeing. Fibre naturally fills you up. Consequently, you are unlikely to overeat as you will naturally feel full when your body has had the right amount of goodness. You might notice that a bowl of porridge (complex carbohydrate) fills you up, but a bowl of cornflakes (simple carbohydrate) for example, might not, even though they have the same calories... so don't be fooled into thinking that fewer calories equals more healthy! Balance is the key. It's important to have a lot of fibre in your diet as it guards against obesity, bowel cancer and diabetes. The goodness is found in nuts, fruits, seeds and most importantly (which are removed in refined and processed carbohydrates), the outer grain coating and skins. Bran is a perfect form of fibre. You can add nuts to your cereal (keep the skins on though, to keep the goodness) in the morning to get more fibre. Soluble fibre, like bran (can be broken down easily in water) aids digestion because it is easily broken down and helps to clear your system by pushing other food through your digestive system.

Glycaemic Index

It's important to be aware of the types of foods you eat, especially sugar and sugar levels, as it is this, your body fuel that directly affects your emotional state, wellbeing and mood as well as your fat levels and appearance. One way of becoming aware of sugar levels in food is to take a look at the Glycaemic Index. You will start to see a correlation in your various energy levels and the different types of foods on it. The Glycaemic Index was originally used to help diabetics control their blood sugar levels and it can also give you a rough idea of the types of carbohydrates and sugar levels that you consume and the level of 'goodness' contained within them. The scale basically measures carbohydrates and how they affect your blood sugar level and thus, your insulin level. The higher the GI value on the index, the more it releases sugar, at a quicker rate into the bloodstream, which in turn raises your insulin levels. It is your insulin and sugar levels that drastically affect your long and short term health as well as your daily energy level. You may start to notice that if you eat lots of food from the upper end of the scale that you do not feel a sustained release of energy to help you through your day, but have an erratic energy level. You will also be suffering from exceptionally high insulin production and blood sugar levels, which is a health risk. As always, moderation is key. Some diets also encourage you to eat high amounts of carbohydrates and low amounts of fat; again, this is not healthy. Although you may seem to lose weight, this is only a short term fix and will damage your health and body in the long term and not give you what you need to live at your optimum level, because it will increase your insulin and blood sugar level too.

I strongly encourage you to get a copy of the Glycaemic Index, which you can easily find online or from your local GP. Below is a selection of foods with various GI levels, to give you a rough idea. It's important that you remember that these foods and their "GI" level will directly affect your energy levels and emotional state… the old saying, "you are what you eat" does indeed have a lot of truth in it.

Foods with a very high GI level

Most processed cereals (cornflakes, for example)
White bread
White rice

Juice
Sweets
Mangos
Raisins

Foods with a high GI level

Cake
Some biscuits
Baked beans
Pasta
Potatoes
Peas
Oranges
Muesli

Foods with a medium GI level

Porridge
Rye Bread
Skimmed milk
Low fat yoghurts
Barley
Brown rice
Pitta bread
Chickpeas
Lentils

Kidney beans
Apples
Beetroot

Foods with a low GI level

Fish
Seafood
Chicken and Meats
Eggs
Green vegetables
Yoghurt
Milk
Cottage cheese
Soya beans
Plums
Grapefruit
Nuts

Insulin

Your body's insulin level is directly related to what you eat and it is very important as it not only has a major effect on your appetite but also on your body fat level as well as metabolism and other important bodily functions. The hormone is secreted by your pancreas and its most important role is to balance and regulate glucose (sugar) in your blood and body. It is insulin that regulates the level of sugar in your blood stream. And the level is directly affected by your intake of food because your food is broken down (digested) into blood sugar so that it can be directly absorbed and used by the body. If you eat high levels of sugar that are of no use to your body, it is still forced to secrete high levels of insulin to deal with it and absorb it into the body. A fluctuating blood level is not healthy at all and directly affects your cravings and feelings of hunger as well as your mood. The imbalance is perpetuated as your body will secrete even more insulin, which will not have the desired effect on the body as it becomes desensitised to it… and even more will be needed. Obviously, this can cause diabetes, heart disease, hypoglycaemia and obesity. The main causes are unhealthy consumption of simple carbohydrates and foods that register high on the GI index. Also, it's interesting to note, that it is these foods which give you the least nourishment because they contain the highest levels of 'empty calories', which will only fill you up temporarily and leave you feeling empty and hungry, with little nutritional value. As we have already discussed, you should try to eat complex carbohydrates because these will give you real energy as they are rich in nutrients and fibre. They are the ones with a lower GI level so raise the blood sugar levels in a sustained more healthy way. If you want to feel great, it is these that you should be incorporating into your diet. You will see real positive changes in your mood and emotional state if you switch from the refined processed carbohydrates like white rice, cereals, white bread, sweets and cakes to the complex carbohydrates.

Carbohydrates: Mood and Wellbeing

Your mood is directly affected by the levels of noradrenaline and serotonin in your body. These neurotransmitters have a big effect on your wellbeing and mental state and are mainly derived from carbohydrates. Some carbohydrates, like simple carbohydrates, give you a temporary high, because they quickly raise your blood sugar levels and it is this fluctuation that induces a quick burst of serotonin that might temporarily feel great. The problem is that when the insulin starts to regulate your blood level, your serotonin level will also begin to drop and you will start to feel 'down' and this directly affects your mood in a negative way, which of course affects behaviour. This behaviour will probably result in more chocolate and sweets!

It's a self-perpetuating cycle that will need to be broken and *can* be broken. You will feel so much better if you have sustained serotonin high; you will feel great throughout the day, without the downs and chocolate withdrawal symptoms, if you eat foods like turkey breast, tuna and other high protein foods which contain the essential amino acids.

Practical carbohydrate advice, give it a try!

- Try to eat foods that have a low GI level.
- Stay away, as much as you can, from simple carbohydrates.
- When you snack, try and snack on vegetables and fruits that have a low GI level.
- Look for foods that are naturally high in fibre like whole grains and fresh vegetables.
- Mix and combine your carbohydrates with proteins and other essential fats.

Proteins

Protein makes up every part of your body, including your bones, blood, skin, nails and muscles. Your body is made up of mostly water, but after that comes protein. Protein is the foundation of your body and its growth and repair mechanisms. From bones, teeth, to the regeneration of tissue, it is the basic building block of your body and it also helps maintain your hormonal system as well as strengthen your immune system. It is the foundation of what makes you.

Good Protein Foods

Turkey breast
Chicken breast
Tuna
Trout
Lamb
Eggs

Cottage cheese
Whey
Soya products
Sardines
Cod

I would personally advise, that for a normal healthy diet, you steer clear of the protein shakes and various types of powders and supplements unless they are used as part of a healthy balanced diet and lifestyle and with your GP's advice. Especially those weight training who might use them as part of a special diet. Also, if you have a diet that is based on shakes and drinks, then this is very unhealthy. You may experience short term weight loss, but they will not provide you with the essential fatty acids and calories that you need as well as running the risk of developing serious health problems. Any weight lost will probably be muscle tissue as opposed to fat, very short term, and possibly detrimental to your health.

Healthy Amino Acids

There are twenty-three amino acids in the body. Protein is broken down into amino acids and absorbed into the blood. These amino acids have various functions in the body. Eight of the twenty-three amino acids are essential, and these are necessary and need to be in the food that we eat so that they can be used as building blocks for the vital proteins in the body.

Protein: Mood and Wellbeing

Your mood and emotional state are determined by various neurotransmitters. These are powerful messengers that deliver signals to various parts of the body, determining how you feel at any given point. Amino acids are integral in the formation of neurotransmitters which directly change your mood. These include:

Acetylcholine

Acetylcholine is responsible for helping you think clearly and improving your mental awareness.

Adrenaline

This hormone kicks in in high-stress scenarios, when you might need to react quickly and gives you what you need to react decisively.

Dopamine and Noradrenaline

Dopamine and Noradrenaline are neurotransmitters that give you the feeling of control.

Gamma-aminobutyric acid

A relaxant neurotransmitter.

Serotonin

Serotonin level has a direct effect on mood. Low levels can cause feelings of depression. Your body produces serotonin using various amino acids (specifically, tryptophan) found in foods like turkey breast, bananas and fish.

Practical Protein Advice

We need to have a diet that includes all of the essential amino acids to perform to our maximum capabilities. It is important to note that not all proteins contain them. Beans, lentils, nuts, seed and pulses, often called 'incomplete proteins' as they do not. Nevertheless, a healthy combination of all types in combination with food like grain, rice or soya will give you all the protein that your body needs. Not necessarily in the same meal together though, because you can spread it out over the day and still get the same nourishment and energy. A quick and simple way of determining how much protein to eat in your meal is to take a look at the palm of your hand. The protein in your meal should cover your palm and ideally be the same thickness too. This is quite an accurate indicator of your optimum amount of protein in a meal. You generally should eat one gram of protein for every kilogram of your body weight. A quick protein snack is the best way to get full and energised over a long period. You could try a small can of tuna, sardines or even a hard-boiled egg. A really tasty option is to combine your protein with carbohydrates and essential fats, like chicken or turkey breast slices a vegetable dip or vegetable small cuts.

Other protein suggestions:

- Eat lots of oily fish like sardines, mullet, salmon and mackerel as they contain essential fatty acids (Omegas 3 and 6) which will improve your general wellbeing and prevent conditions like heart disease.
- If you're vegetarian then you have a wide variety to choose from including, cheeses (low

fat), soya products, eggs, beans, seeds, tofu and pulses. Combine grains with your source of protein in the meal to complete it. Or you could try pasta, brown rice, wholemeal bread with chickpeas, lentils or stir-fried tofu with rice or vegetables and a soya product, for a great protein combination.

- Try to eat protein foods that are organic and fresh. Grass-fed meats and organic poultry contain more nutrients, which mean that you will get more goodness from less mass.

Fats

Not all fats are bad! You can sit down to eat a really large low fat, healthy looking meal and still feel empty afterwards and unsatisfied. It's usually at this point that we turn to a packet of crisps or a bar of chocolate to fill that gap... and as the rest of the meal was really healthy, that would be alright, right? No. Your body does indeed need fat. The important thing is that you eat the right fats and the right amounts of fat...as opposed to chocolates and sweets. You will only feel satisfied and full if your body has the fuel to function at its optimum, and that fuel is derived from the essential fats, that your body needs.

Fat is a very important energy source for the body... so don't get carried away with 'low fat' foods as this can be misleading. Those kind souls won't tell you what type of fat, it's 'low' in, and that is the key (and the rest of the really unhealthy stuff they've packed in there...a stone in the street has low fat, but you wouldn't eat that!). Fat is an integral part of our protective system, especially protecting our internal organs and has other important functions, like in the production of the hormones like testosterone, oestrogen, and progesterone. Fat also transports these hormones around the body and carries vitamins A, E, D and K as well as other fat-soluble minerals. Fat also helps maintain your weight (the right type and amounts), because it decreases your appetite, so that you eat less because you don't feel hungry.

Different Types of Fat

There are two types of fat. Saturated fat comes from cream, butter, meat, dripping and is derived from animals. It is very concentrated and is solid at room temperature. Unsaturated fats (polyunsaturated and monounsaturated) come from the earth (plants, for example). Like olive oils, vegetable oils (sunflower, rapeseed oils, safflower and flaxseed oils) as well as nut oils. That said, it can also be derived from oily fish, like tuna, mackerel and sardines. You can tell an unsaturated fat because it is liquid at normal room temperature.

Important Fatty Acids

Your central nervous system, reproductive and immune systems are all supported by essential fatty acids that are broken down from the fat that you eat. In fact, they are so important that every cell within your body will need an appropriate amount just to function properly. The fat that you eat is broken down into fatty acids and glycerol and also protects you against illness and has lots of other important functions. The basic molecular structure of fatty acids consists of 'arms' that attach themselves to carbons and hydrogens. The crucial difference between saturated and unsaturated forms is that unsaturated fatty acids contain a slightly lower number of bonds, making them looser and hence liquid at room temperature. Unsaturated fat can artificially be saturated with hydrogen and this process is called hydrogenation, creating hydrogenated fat. It's advisable to stay away from hydrogenated fat, because the body finds it difficult to metabolise, which means that it will just be stored as visible fat. You will find hydrogenated fat in foods like low fat spreads, biscuits, pastries, cereal bars and packaged foods. The process is not good for your body as the fat is artificially changed from a liquid into a solid by adding hydrogen, turning it into a semi-solid. Yes… that's the stuff you eat! It has been said that this *stuff* can cause cancer, birth disorders, heart disease and even low testosterone in men. You'll find it in some spreads and margarine, as well as some vegetable oils, which directly adversely affect your body, your cholesterol levels and ability to metabolise essential fatty acids.

You can eat small amounts of saturated fat like, butter and cream but it's not a good idea or a healthy one, to eat hydrogenated fats, in fact, you should try and cut them out completely from your diet. You need to include unsaturated fats into your diet and specifically more of the polyunsaturated type. Beware that hydrogenated fats are usually found (and hidden!) in foods like biscuits, breaded foods, salad creams, kinds of margarine, various sauces, cakes, pastries, pasties, pies and things like fish fingers, and many others. Try to stick to polyunsaturated fat (or at least include unsaturated fats into your diet), and stay well away from hydrogenated fats. Unsaturated fats, and specifically polyunsaturated, contains two very important essential fatty acids, Omega 3 and Omega 6. Omega 3 and Omega 6 are recommended to be consumed on a very regular basis. They are great for keeping your weight down because they act as natural indicators, preventing you from feeling the need to eat more than necessary and they produce cholecystokinin which also tells the brain that you are satisfied and full, so you don't even feel the need to overeat, or want to. They also help in burning fat so that it is not stored visibly. That fat is used as energy so that you feel great, as opposed to round the belly, which doesn't feel so great! Omega 3 also has a positive effect on insulin in the body and in blood regulation. You can find polyunsaturated fat in oily fish, which are very good for you, like sardines, mackerel as well as in grains, nuts, vegetables, seeds and also hempseed oil and flaxseed oil.

Practical Fat Advice

- Include oily fish into your diet.
- Eat foods that contain unsaturated fats.
- Use olive oil for cooking.
- Try not to heat oils as they tend to lose nutritional value.
- Instead of frying foods, why not try and grill, boil or bake.
- When you buy meat, try and buy lean organic meat/poultry.

- Get rid of all hydrogenated fats in your diet.
- Try not to eat processed foods and takeaways like hamburgers and fries, fish and chips, curries etc.
- If you like curries then go for lamb tikka, a dry dish or chicken tandoori.
- Eat oils that contain essential fatty acids like Omega 3 and 6 and add them to your salad and dressings. Try lemon juice, red or white wine vinegar or garlic instead of butter. Try and add flaxseed, olive, or hempseed oil to your vegetables instead of other spreads.
- When you buy oil make sure that you keep the cap screwed on tightly so that it is airtight. Keep them in a cool dark place like the fridge, and try and purchase glass containers that are dark. Flaxseed oil should be kept refrigerated at all times.

How to Feel Energised

A lot of people comment on my energy level. People say that when they're around me that they themselves feel energised! I feel energised just saying the word ENERGY!

Energy is excitement! Now…we all love to meet

energetic (sane!) people. Energetic people are attractive; you want to be around them. They give you something. They can raise your spirits when you're down or had a long day at work or just aren't in the mood. They give you something. Just in the same way as negative, tired people usually drain your energy and can make you feel bad. Negative energy spreads. Positive energy spreads, we all have the ability to affect other people and to determine how people see us and ultimately treat us.

Have you noticed that if you smile, people usually smile back at you? Also, when you're feeling down have you ever tried smiling (I know it might sound crazy but it works!). Just the physical activity alone can cause a positive emotional response. It's called positive thinking, and it works, but the key factor in all of this is your physical body. How do you actually feel? With your personal development, it's important that you're honest with yourself. It's quite easy to fool the world and yourself into thinking anything, but at the end of the day, positive personal growth will come with honesty and logical steps.

Some people seem really happy and energetic on the surface and look great but inside are feeling drained, overworked, overstretched and running on empty. This is actually very common.

How do I change that?

Start with your body. Implement what you've read and you will see your energy level transform!

Water, Food, Exercise, Sleep

Drink Water.

Water is the body's most important nutrient. If you do not drink enough water your body will begin to retain water as an emergency measure and you'll dehydrate. Even mild dehydration can sap your energy and make you tired. Did you know that the body can survive for up to five weeks without food but only five days without water? The minimum recommendation of water intake is eight glasses per day and twice that for active individuals. Drink water as much as possible and as frequently as possible. You should be sipping water as you're reading this! If you want to feel energised then drink a glass of water as soon as you wake in the morning. One of those big ones. Gulp that thing down! It's a quick and easy way to get your day going in a healthy and energised way. Similarly, gulp a glass down before you go to bed. Think about it. During your time in bed, your body is using up your water supply to regulate your body's temperature as well as continue to provide the fluid environment for normal cell metabolism, turgor (structure and form of the body), sweat. It's important to replenish your supply as soon as possible. Increase your water intake and you'll see higher energy levels throughout the day.

Tip: Make sure that it is clean, clear water! (Room temperature is best and tap water is fine) Beer, wine, vodka and cola etc. don't count!

You are made up of 60% water, which is two-thirds of your body. Your brain is made of more than 50% water. Small changes in your fluid intake can have drastic positive effects on your wellbeing and quality of life. Water is vital to the intracellular and extracellular functioning of your body (inside your cells, and outside, like in your saliva and blood plasma) and it's also found in vegetables and fruits (which contain about 90% water). Not only will water cleanse your body of all the waste materials and metabolic residual, but it will also give you a full satisfied feeling if you have a glass before your meal, as well as after. Water is absolutely calorie free, but don't be fooled by all of the various bottled water and sweetened drinks that usually have a lot of sugar added to them and are calorie packed (usually with pure sugar).

A very good way to see if you are drinking enough water is to take a look at your urine when you go to the toilet. It should be clear and colourless. It is essential to drink water, especially before, during and after dancing and exercise, you need to keep hydrated. You tend to perspire a lot when you exercise (as well as naturally through the day) and this can lead to fatigue and dehydration. This is easily combated by drinking lots of water. Although I recommend pure water, you can also drink fruit teas, herbal teas as well as some diluted juices. If you work in an office then you should keep a big bottle of water under your table all day and cut down on the coffee. Coffee, a stimulant and a diuretic, is full of caffeine and actually pushes water out of your body, like alcohol, which is a packed carbohydrate and full of empty calories.

- Keep alcohol and coffee to a minimum.
- Invest in a filter or purchase bottled water, if possible.
- Drink eight or more glasses of water per day.
- If you drink pure fruit juices (from

concentrate), why not try diluting them with water.

- Keep alcohol to a minimum. Try not to drink more than one or two glasses of wine per day.
- Why not investigate the delicious variety of fresh vegetable juices that are out there? Carrot juice is one of my favourites, and extremely tasty and healthy.
- Green teas are said to aid weight loss by speeding up the body's burning of fat. Drink it in moderation though because it does contain caffeine.

Healthy Eating

We have all heard the saying "you are what you eat" and it makes absolute sense. You wouldn't expect your car to run efficiently without petrol, so you'd expect that we all need our petrol too, and to run at our best we need the good stuff! Basically, that means a healthy balanced diet, and it's essential for good health, high energy levels and for you to work (and play) at your optimum level. The key word is BALANCED. Eating the right amounts of proteins, carbohydrates and fats in your meals will not only leave you feeling energised throughout the day but also naturally speeds up the fat burning process. Put simply, you can get into shape faster, without the need for quick fix crackpot dieting schemes! Balanced meals cause a hormonal response within the body, which results in burning stored body fat. This is good news for people who like to eat normal food although as you'd expect, moderation is key also. I've already outlined what types of food is good to eat, so feel free to go through and underline and pick and choose what you feel is right for you. It's only important that you take care of the basics. There is no need for a strict health regime, with no room for enjoyment.

Enjoy plenty of whole grains, fruits and vegetables. Eat regular meals. Remember to eat five portions of fruit or vegetables every day and to keep your intake of fizzy drinks, crisps and sweets to a minimum. Eat breakfast! Quite simple and easy to enjoy.

Summary: What To Eat

We are all different types of people with different metabolic rates. We are all unique and what works for one may not necessarily work for all, so it is important that you discover what works for you and what you feel doesn't. I'm going to summarise what we've been through and it's really important to take note if you are tempted by all of the crazy diets out there, especially the low fat, high carbohydrates diets or the other temporary quick fix diets that can seriously damage your health. It's really quite simple. Moderation is the key to a healthy body. A healthy balance of carbohydrates, proteins and essential fats are essential for a successful healthy body with lots of energy! It might take a little effort to focus and think about the foods which you consume, but the reward in the improvement of your quality of life will be worth it. It is also a decision that you choose to make, to live in a healthy way, and turn away from quick fixes that don't work. It's a worthwhile lifestyle choice that you have to make for yourself.

Try and eat foods that rate low on the GI Index and increase your fruit and vegetable intake, for a better source of carbohydrate.

Eat a healthy moderation of grains too. If you choose foods that rate low on the GI Index, as part of a balanced diet, you will find yourself feeling full and satisfied a lot more, with high energy. Try to increase your protein intake, which you can get from a balanced amount of meat, fish and eggs. A palm-sized amount of complete protein with each meal, and try and eat fish at least three times a week, especially oily fish with Omega 3 and 6. This will help you to feel full and satisfied and will increase your cells' sensitivity to insulin.

If you want to lose weight, make sure that you eat foods that have a low GI and are high in fibre, so that you feel full. It's important that insulin and energy are released slowly in your body, and this feeling of wellbeing can be attained by combining carbohydrates and proteins with a small amount of healthy fat. Eat when you feel hungry and stop when you feel full. If you have a snack then try and combine carbohydrates, fats and proteins, like vegetable sticks and healthy dips, nuts, meat and vegetables. Forget counting calories, as you will get all you need and have an overall feeling of wellbeing, as well as keep your weight down by eating a common sense balanced diet. If you do cut your calories then you may feel tired throughout the day, as you're not getting the goodness you need and your metabolism may slow down. If you feel the need to eat. Think about what kind of food you eat…that is the key. You can eat fat: make sure that it's the right kind. Try to keep away from saturated fat, but try olive oils, safflower and flaxseed oils. If you're one who especially craves chocolate or sweets, you can solve that by incorporating low GI foods into your diet, as well. Finally, if you have any metabolic problems or concerns about your health then immediately book an appointment and go and have a chat with your local GP or an accredited nutritionist who will be able to give you suitable advice catered to suit your needs especially if you have an intolerance to certain foods etc.

General Fitness

Exercise can be fun! And it's essential that you exercise regularly so that you can keep in shape as well as feel amazing! It doesn't have to be boring or even in a gym (or dance studio for that matter!) There are many, many ways to keep fit and dancing is just one of many that are great, a lot of fun, and stimulating for the mind as well as body. You need to exercise to keep your body functioning to its optimum level. It boosts your metabolism, keeps your stress levels down and keeps you in great shape. Your state of mind will be drastically altered for the better. Regular exercise gives you a natural high and promotes a healthy lifestyle that will be reflected in your appearance and enjoyment of life. Again, it's a case of making a conscious decision to change your life for the better. You will have to commit to regular exercise and keep at it, to see real results and you will get better at it, and enjoy it more, the more you do it and keep it up. Dancing is the best way to keep in shape in my opinion. It's fun, and you burn lots of calories and will give your body tone, especially your legs. It doesn't matter what style either. As long as you're moving to the music. In fact, try no style at all! As long as you're moving your body then that is a great start and a great way to keep in shape! One hour of dancing can burn about 350 calories… and you can smile while you're at it too!

Look Great!

It's important if you want to look trim, that you burn calories so that you get rid of any excess body fat. The more you exercise, the more you boost your metabolic rate, which is the rate that you burn energy.

Your Body's Make Up

The more muscle you have, the more calories you will burn and your muscles are metabolically active even when you're relaxing. Males usually have a higher metabolism than females because they have bigger muscles (generally). Inactivity is the killer. If you want to keep fit, then you have to perpetuate your youth by exercising. Your metabolic rate peaks in your early twenties and gently declines after that until at around thirty years old you start to lose muscle mass and your body fat might increase at a quicker rate… so it's important to keep exercising. If you don't, then your muscles will lose their shape and decrease in size too. This can be combated by regular, natural exercise, and you'll feel great in no time.

Boost your Metabolism

- Put your music on loud, and dance around the house!
- Walk, walk, walk! Do you really need to drive locally? If you do, be aware of where you park the car and try and park at the furthest part of the car park so that you can walk and get some exercise that way.
- Save your pound coin, dash the trolley and try carrying the shopping to the car
- Invest in a pair of comfortable trainers (sneakers)
- Get a bicycle… it's a real investment
- A very good way to keep fit is to stop taking the escalators and lifts: take the stairs! This is great for your legs and will get easier the more you do it
- After you've eaten, why not go out for a

quick brisk walk

- Get active… leave the remote control and jump up and change the channel manually
- Housework can help you burn up 170 calories per hour! Make sure you pump the music up and clean with big movements, keep to the rhythm too
- Become more active by walking and moving about more, and not being lazy! Swap automatic for manual (like lawnmowers for example)

See, you can improve your health by making small easy changes that don't involve a lot of conscious effort…and small changes like this can make a lot of difference to your health and lifestyle. It's a good start if you want to start somewhere

Dance and Aerobic fitness

If you want to improve your aerobic fitness and overall wellbeing then you'll have to start using the big muscles in your body and get them moving, with large movements… dancing is perfect, but not the only way to do it! Your aerobic fitness is your ability to deliver oxygen to your working muscles and the cardiovascular system's ability to do it with ease. The more you do it, the better you will get at it and the better you will feel. You will get a metabolic boost, as your body and muscles encourage your heart and lungs to work harder and faster, to keep up with your demand. With regular exercise, you'll become naturally toned and burn fat naturally and effectively and start to look and feel great.

Aerobic exercise will improve your physicality, your wellbeing, your appearance, give you a stronger heart and lungs, improve your posture and composure, release and relieve stress, give you psychological wellbeing, stronger bones and so much more! Aerobic exercise is very important and it should be regular, with at least three thirty minute sessions per week. It's also important that it is high intensity; that you focus on what you are doing and your muscles. This may be a quick walk for some people, but a fast running or sprint workout for another. It is relative, but a great indicator is your sweat levels... you need to sweat. Dancing is the perfect aerobic activity because not only does it give you a great physical workout, but also a mental workout. It really does get easier as you do it, and as we've already looked at previously, it's never usually a physical issue in the real world which prevents advancement in dance or in any physical activity, but mental barriers that can be removed with a little effort. So, in the words of Nike: *Just do it!*

Part 3

Dance and Physical Expression

The Aesthetics of Dance

Don't worry about the title of the chapter... all shall be explained. When I look at a piece of choreography or any movement at all I look specifically at the shape of the body and the manner in which certain movements are executed. If you think about it, even something as simple as walking down the street, turning to wave at your friend and then stopping for a quick chat is a pretty complex piece of choreography (when you break it down). Importantly, it is completely natural. You would never think twice about the way in which the manoeuvre was executed because it would be completely second nature to you. You would not have to think consciously about breaking down each step that you took; the way in which you stealthily pivoted on your heel for the turn and the swift raised arm that you coincided perfectly with the drop of your head and a smile. It's a completely natural, perfectly rhythmic piece of choreography.

Defining Good and Bad Dancing

I would say that there is indeed a universal law that links movement and its execution, to what is judged to be aesthetically pleasing. In fact, it is quite obvious to me that we artists must utilise 'the law', first with understanding and then with the application of it to the dance and choreography – or any other type of movement, form of human expression or art. As a result, we can capture that magic that permeates through our whole existence. Both through the physical world as well as purposefully, through great art and architecture for thousands, if not millions of years.

Essentially, I am talking about GEOMETRY, LINES and MATHEMATICS and how this applies to AESTHETICS, STANCE, POISE and. MAJESTY: a perfectly executed dance move that is pleasing to the eye, to the dancer, to the choreographer and captivates the observer by its natural elegance and beauty. The key is to try and understand WHAT makes the art piece so aesthetically pleasing. Is it a coincidence? Probability? Random chaos? Or is it linked to some kind of universal law or force? In relation to your body and dance, it's important to be aware of what

I like to call your 'body lines'. Body lines incorporate the idea that the beauty of the choreography or movement should be conveyed through positioning and elegant execution of moves along with your natural body lines, and within certain geometric parameters, that exist and have already been studied for thousands of years, and adjudged to be aesthetically pleasing.

Now is not the time to go into depth, but I will highlight two important lines of the body that you should be aware of and the importance of working within them and also how that awareness can transform your physicality and dancing ability. I am essentially talking about proportion and certain geometric ratios such as the 'Golden Ratio' or 'Divine Proportion' as the ancient Greeks called it, or 'Fibonacci', after the Italian Mathematician, Leonardo of Pisa. It is important that you become aware of your body and its lines, as well as how to implement a dance step through those lines. At the very least, the fact that you are aware of your body will translate quite clearly in your poise and physicality. At the end of the day, you are a mover and you may want to be a dancer. It follows that you are using your body and therefore it is important to understand your physicality so that you can utilise shape and form in your dance. Shape and form are what dance and expression are all about.

I remember exactly when proportion and alignment and its relation to the human body came to my attention. I was about seven years old and captivated by a picture that I didn't understand at the time, but knew that it was very interesting. Leonardo Da Vinci's drawing 'Vitruvian Man' intrigued me even then and still does, even more so, now. He understood the body and its lines, the aesthetic beauty contained in the very specific geometry and how that can be translated into art, and does indeed flow through all of nature. I say that a dancer should utilise this knowledge even at a basic level; flowing through the lines while executing any given move and at the very least appreciate the beauty of the human body.

A wonky building, with uneven sides, not only looks wrong but will eventually fall, but a solid geometrical shape will remain strong and always retain a certain beauty that is clear to see. Dance is no different; I do not differentiate between the human physical movement to rhythm and the various kinds of sacred architecture or great art, from the renaissance or any other time in history, which are quite obviously linked to sacred and complex mathematical ratios and the geometry hidden within. In fact, as a choreographer, I feel that 'alignment' and even a kind of 'sacred geometry' that is observed throughout the universe, which has been understood and incorporated into art by numerous great philosophers and artists, should be all the more observed and incorporated in varying degrees, into dance. At that stage, we shall indeed see magic and the power of the body as well as the spirit manifesting in a truly glorious performance.

Divine Proportion

'Phi' is a sound and the 21st letter of the Greek alphabet; it is a number (1.618…), but specifically a very important number with unique properties. It is a number and proportion which renaissance artists called 'Divine Proportion'. The mathematician Luca Pacioli published *De Divina Proportione* in 1509, where he investigated and explored the relationship between mathematical proportion and the visually stimulating and aesthetically pleasing. He was a trained artist and a friend of Leonardo Da Vinci. The book had a massive influence on future artists, architects and those interested in visual expression. It was Leonardo Da Vinci who seemed to promote the idea that the human body was also linked to the Golden Ratio, he also illustrated the book. It is clear, although keenly debated, that he incorporated it in his other works, like the Mona Lisa and other amazing pieces that are known for their amazing beauty. It is likely that he, and other great artists before him, as well as since (Mondrian and Salvador Dalí for example) have proportioned their art, paintings, sculpture, architecture and man-made beauty according to the golden ratio and other proportions. Interestingly, the golden ratio proportion can be seen in many of the most magnificent and beautiful creations ever constructed. The Egyptians used it in the creation of the pyramids. The ancient Greeks were guided by it in the construction of the Acropolis and it was also used later in the design of the Notre Dame Cathedral in Paris.

Whatever this 'magic proportion' is, it is not only restricted to man-made objects. It is found in nature, throughout the human body, plants, space and the proportions of the planets, music and the arts and throughout the whole universe. The

German intellectual Adolph Zeising (1810-1876) who researched exhaustively into the link between the golden ratio and man-made objects as well as in nature wrote, in 1854:

"[A universal law] in which is contained the ground-principle of all formative striving for beauty and completeness in the realms of both nature and art, and which permeates, as a paramount spiritual ideal, all structures, forms and proportions, whether cosmic or individual, organic or inorganic, acoustic or optical; which finds its fullest realisation, however, in the human form"

It is quite clear that aesthetic beauty and geometric proportion are linked in a very special way, some might even say in a spiritual way. The initiated have propagated this through masterpieces for centuries and I am in total agreement. Form and proportion are fundamentals in dance and it is essential that in conveying real artistic beauty, this is not forgotten. It is not only an integral part in an artistic sense but also in a way of maximising and utilising strength too. Stance has always been important; we just need to take a look toward the east and the various martial arts to get a sense of that. The 'Hachiji dachi' stance in karate is based on the Kanji; the shape for the number 8, in Japanese writing and it is thought to specifically maximise strength. This is very important to grasp. A certain stance or position maximises your physical strength and ability to perform the next step effectively. It is also believed by some, that certain stances also enhance the spirit and allow it to flow freely through the movement.

Any great artist in history, from Leonardo Da Vinci to John Lennon has spoken about this in other ways, they often expressed that they were just vessels and that the magic just flowed into them and through them, and that they were there to capture it at that particular time. The key is to be available at the time and to be accepting of the magic when it does eventually arrive. It's also very important that you, as the reader, understand that great artists do not think in categories and boxes. Something that is aesthetically beautiful is beautiful; whatever label you want to place on it, a great piece of music is a great piece of music, no matter what you want to call it. Likewise, an amazing piece of choreography, a karate stance, or the poise of a leopard, before it attacks or even the design of a building are all beautiful physical expressions. It is that simple. They are all linked.

The labels that we give different kinds of physical expression usually serve to divide us from them, or at the very least, serve as a psychological divide, that can prevent us from appreciating them or taking a look and considering them in the first place.

It's quite interesting that a label, like a value, is just an idea. Nothing more, an idea in someone's head… and quite usually a barrier…which is interesting when you think about it. Imagine the freedom, enjoyment and experience that might be gained if we dropped a lot of them and just absorbed and appreciated things as they really were, good or bad, right or wrong.

Let's take a look at a couple of examples. One of the most frequent questions that I get asked as a choreographer is, "What style do you dance?" Now, that is a very interesting question, because the short answer should be "any style that I choose, at any given time". If I choose to take a ballet step and incorporate it with a hip-hop step, and then change the dynamics of the piece by fusing it with a spice of jazz and pinch a few of the swinging upper arm movements from the masked native American Indians in Alaska. What do you call that style? Why does it need a name in the first place? I will give it a try, without fear or restricting labels or names (in somebody else's head) and if it works then great…and if not, no big deal! We are free to express ourselves!

On the other hand, one might find the greatest urban street dancer on the planet, right in the middle of the city and try and convey the beauty of a demi-pointe to him without success due to the stigma attached to ballet in that particular location. It is when great minds do start to think outside the box, without the labels and prejudices, that amazing ground-breaking human expressions start to happen.

Just think of the moonwalk! Think about it, what is the moonwalk composed of exactly? A fusion of demi-pointe and a raw slide from the street, perhaps? Again, somebody must have just tried it out and had a unique idea. Michael Jackson too, for example, fuses every style out there in his short movies. You might have a jazz dancer who watches Michael dance in 'The Way You Make Me Feel' or 'Beat it' and say to themselves "I could never do that", but in actual fact, every step from those two particular videos was derived directly from the jazz/ballet

Broadway musical *West Side Story*. Yes… every choreographed step!

Now that same dancer would have no difficulty at all with the steps from *West Side Story*. Now that is not logical at all! Again, the problem arises, not from the reality of the situation and the dancer's actual ability, but from the dancer's mind and from the application of labels.

These labels prevent honest consideration, simple learning and simply executing the moves.

I'll say it again: great artists and thinkers do not think in terms of categories or labels! They are merely marketing ploys, most of the time anyway. A commercial initiative separate from the art, as a means of reaching (a polite way of saying 'selling to') more people who are only comfortable consuming in the average pigeon hole way. It should be irrelevant to the artist or thinker as it often prevents artistic growth (or just human growth for that matter). If you think or attempt to create with the shackles of self-restriction you will never reach your full potential. You have capped your talent level from the outset: the main point of this book!

You may be getting my point already… I do not differentiate between a choreographed dance sequence and a random physical reaction and movement to something in the street. The only difference between a preconceived dance step or a so-called piece of choreography and random physical action is the intention. In fact, the beauty contained within that random unplanned set of movements has the ability to far exceed the beauty of a pre-planned set of movements any day! Why? Because it is an honest natural expression of who we are, without the conscious fear, doubt and restriction that we as people in this system place upon ourselves every day.

The key word is 'honesty', followed by 'natural'. Nature and the natural are where the beauty lies. If you've ever observed the amazing herds of wildebeest in Africa and various animals or a flock of birds migrating, you'd be awestruck by the seemingly choreographed totally cohesive movement and 'dance' that is performed. Literal perfection and beauty that we humans can only aspire to reproduce on the stage or in any artistic capacity. That said, it is interesting that a herd by definition is unstructured; however, if you look closely at the movement and observe, you might just notice a few leading animals. They are copied by the rest of the herd; they 'choreograph' this beautiful scene and direct the others. Technically this particular animal is called the 'control animal' and it is they that choreograph this natural spectacle. It is a truly amazing feat. Would it be too much, I ask to study the movements of wildebeest or flying birds and incorporate them into your art or dance? Not at all! Why wouldn't that be one of the first places to search for inspiration in the first place?

The truly great minds have been doing this for thousands of years because they have understood the link between nature and aesthetically pleasing man-made creations. Of course, that we are natural beings that inhabit the earth and are linked to it in every way is especially relevant. I would also highlight the bridge between what we view as 'out there' or as 'irrelevant to us', for it might sometimes be a lot more significant than we might imagine. We often ignore and overlook such scientific connections that are totally relevant to our growth, our art and our lives because we prejudge them away, to our loss. Even the beauty of a herd of animals is closely linked in physical movement, responses and emotional behaviour to human beings that it would certainly shock some people. Human phenomena and behaviours like fashion 'fads', popular 'crazes', stock market crashes, flash riots, religious movements and actions can all be attributed to involving 'herd behaviour'. Even down to the physical day-to-day movements of people on the tube, on the streets and around the town. All choreographed, consciously or unconsciously, all natural and all linked to wildebeest roaming the open plains!

The natural choreography that is generally ignored is often the biggest most amazing expression because it is unconscious. I cannot walk around any major city and not be captivated by the sequence of events around me; all this transpires into the most amazing choreographed routine (usually the same one daily, I hasten to add!) around the specifically placed landmarks, that make the stage, as Shakespeare once said. Anybody who has been to Cairo, Egypt will have observed the 'magic in the madness', so to speak, and the beauty in the hustle and bustle and constant horn blowing that create a wonderful, yet very interesting, symphony of noise that you'll never forget.

This can be taken further though. I do not think that it is necessary to restrict yourself in any way at all. I do not think that it is at all essential to differentiate between any type of physical expression (or any other kind of expression) that is aesthetically pleasing (or not for that matter). It is that conscious act of differentiation that, as well as stifling growth, might prevent us from expressing ourselves to our maximum capability before we even start to follow our idea through or our heart or our innermost dreams and desires.

Experiencing different types of supposedly unrelated forms of beauty, and as artists, interpreting them and moulding them for our audience is what a true artist can do; it is amazing what wonderful results can come from this kind of non-linear thought process. It can be a real learning and educational process for all involved. YOU, the reader are the artist and the world is YOUR stage! You are free to express yourself in any way you choose, using anything or any kind of inspiration you choose, at any particular time, for any particular reason. Be it work, play, performance, relaxation, following your dreams, parachuting out of a plane! Whatever! You are free to express yourself. Don't forget that.

A musical note, a dance move, a perfectly structured building, a flower, the planets, a statue, a cat, a dog, an ocean: use them all as your inspiration. Why differentiate between them at all? Why mentally restrict yourself? You are free to think outside the box and outside of your universal schooling and training (which often only encourages linear thinking, and punishes the opposite). You have the ability to think in a non-generic way because you are a unique individual. What an amazing world of beauty, diversity and fulfilment we could live in if we would only unlock the mental restrictions that we have placed on ourselves and walk away from them.

Diversity and seemingly unrelated things are just ideas or concepts in the head. With education and additional information considered, something that might seem unrelated or irrelevant to you might in actual fact, change your whole way of thinking and quality of life or direction. This might have been left unconsidered, or undiscovered due to ignorance or the simple lack of knowledge and understanding. I would say that it's important to free yourself and realise that not only can you learn from all, and incorporate seemingly diverse and unrelated things together as one expression of physical beauty, but if you choose to do so then that is when you will find the most unique kind of fulfilment and magic. True Art!

An expression is expression and you are free to utilise the lot, in your own unique way, if you choose. The American choreographer Wade J Robson, an amazing talent, understood this when he studied the birds migrating. He observed their natural grace and incorporated the movements into his choreography and dance. The pioneer of electronic music, Jean Michel Jarre, understood this when he explained that there is no difference between a sound (e.g. rain hitting the window, a hammer hitting a nail or a car starting) and a musical note, except for the artist's intention.

You are free to express yourself and take inspiration from anywhere you choose. Growing up, one of my favourite pieces of choreography was from Michael Jackson's HIStory world tour and the performance of 'They Don't Care About Us'. It is a montage of various styles but the underpinning theme is a military one. The rebellious nature of the song is reinforced with a thumping drum cadence, the kind of rhythms and beats that have obviously inspired Michael and Janet Jackson through the years and impressed audiences around the world.

The emphatic force, military style and swift movement are unique, inspired and a joy to watch. They recreate that aggression live on stage with the simplicity of the moves in perfect conjunction with the driving beat. Where did the inspiration for this powerful piece of choreography come from? Well, it would seem to me, that it was inspired by a very interesting place indeed. Malaysia… and specifically the Malaysian riot police. The first time I saw it, I knew straight away and noticed the marching simultaneously timed with the raising of the right arm against the left shoulder forcefully, and the slamming of the leg and arm back down, all in unison; it was borrowed from a very unique place.

The Malaysians are known to crack down swiftly on any kind of civil disobedience and they do so with a show of brute force and intimidation. To disperse a crowd they send in the riot police in full gear and a shield in their left hand and a baton in their right hand. While marching forwards in unison, a soldier raises up his baton, in perfect time with his left leg and brings it down thunderously, striking the left-hand side of his shield. It is a very loud and intimidating show of military force but at the same time a rhythmic and choreographed wonder. Tap into that power and incorporate it into a live concert setting to convey a feeling of aggression to the audience.

It is that vision and ability to search and be inspired by the seemingly unrelated, that you too have; the vision that should be free, clear, unfiltered and available to be inspired from all areas and aspects of life without prejudice. It's just a case of unlocking and allowing yourself to think freely...quite simple! You'd be surprised at what you can achieve and the directions that you can travel when you remove the barriers, take away the learned filters and just go with your inner feelings and intuition. I'm not exclusively talking in an artistic sense either; you can apply that same mindset to all aspects of your life.

What is Dance?

Before we take a closer look at ways to improve our dance and movement ability and think about ways to enhance the aesthetic nature of it, I think that it's important to first define and then examine exactly what the word dance means. Technically the word is an expression of human physical movement in a variety of different settings (i.e. performance, social, spiritual) and more precisely is a method of non-verbal communication. It's important to note that dance and music (sound and rhythm) have an obvious symbiotic relationship, and for that reason, I try not to differentiate between them as forms of expression too often. Now, a keyword is movement, which is defined in the dictionary as "the act, process, or result of moving" and even more relevant to us right now, "a particular manner or style of moving", which is simple enough. The usual problem is the manner and style of the movement and how it is interpreted and what differentiates a classy stylised move to a drunken attempt at the same thing!

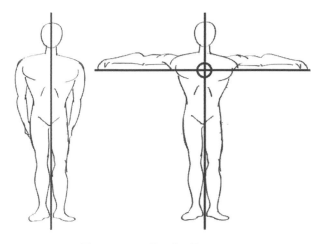

Figure 1: Body Lines

So, it's clear that movement is just moving from point A to point B in an aesthetically pleasing or stylised way. But what exactly makes the move aesthetically pleasing or at least a tolerable physical expression that has some kind of form and that simply put: looks good? I would say that style, form, poise, consistency, timing, placement, control and accuracy are at the top of the list and all make up the concept of aesthetically pleasing execution of movement, in the physical sense. Let's first take a closer look at some of these things and the reasons why it is important to be aware of them and implement some simple techniques to improve them.

Any performer or person who is aware of their own anatomy is in a position of control and can utilise their body in a better way than somebody who is not. It's clear to see when somebody doesn't have this awareness; they may be off balance or look uncomfortable. I also think that it is not important for us all to be experts in anatomy or the optimal balance of weight in our body movements, but the fact that we have a cursory understanding and awareness will help balance and positioning. Just the idea of thinking about your body, standing up straight, head up or executing a movement through a line, will indeed translate to better physicality.

As you can see from Figure 1 your body is made up of lines and it is important that you are aware of them. When you are executing a dance move, think about executing it along the full length consistently, while keeping strictly within the line. The most important line in the body is your centre line (vertical) and secondly your horizontal line through your sternum and arms.

When thinking about our physicality and position the most important aspect is our spine. This means we stand up straight with our head up. Any movement should originate from that centre line consistently unless a step is intended otherwise. It's also important to be aware of your sternum. If you are going to swing your arm to the left, after raising it up, for example, it should originate at the sternum to the left, with a consistent speed, and across and through the line (as outlined in the diagram) without wandering from it (unless it is intended otherwise). The start point of any movement is of importance, as is the endpoint. Some seem to forget that it is the whole movement that is judged. Keep any movement inside your lines (Figure 1), but be aware of the start and end point also. If that start or end point is kept within your obvious straight lines, without wandering out, and is executed with consistency, then it should look great. If you wander from (unless you intend to) a line, to return to it, then this will not look aesthetically pleasing, unless you intended to wander from that line or to make it look a certain way. A straight line is usually the shortest distance between the start of the movement and the end of it and if you think about the various lines in the body and focus on moving your body through them, you should remain balanced and looking great.

Poise

The dictionary definition of poise states that it is a "state of balance, equilibrium or stability" and for obvious reasons, good poise and alignment is the foundation of a good dancer. Posture is where it all begins, so if you want to dance or walk down the street in a straight line, it's important to keep your back straight and lengthened.

Exercise

Find a nice straight wall and go and stand with your back up against it. It is important that you align your feet (heels), your backside (tailbone) as well as your upper back (shoulder blades) completely up against the wall so that you are completely vertical and looking straight ahead as well. This should be your default natural stance. Make sure that you are aware of your stomach and pull it in without holding your breath and using your stomach muscles. It's also important that you relax somewhat, but be aware of your spine and especially your head. Don't let it drop down. At this point you can step away from the wall, making sure that you keep the confident disposition (head up, chest up and a lengthened neck). You now have a reference for good posture and it's important that while you work on improving it you remain aware and constantly re-adjust. Another great way to do this is to place a light book on your head before you step away from the wall and try and keep balanced, while you walk away. It's important to stay focussed and stay balanced. I call this exercise "PEAP": posture and poise equal aesthetically pleasing!

Style

The good dancer understands that it is not about the number of moves you do but in the quality and intensity of the moves you do. Also, importantly, he is not afraid of utilising various dance styles, from tap to street to jazz to ballet. A basic grasp of ballet and jazz is ideal for a dancer but as with verbal communication, the larger your physical dance vocabulary, the more you will be able to communicate physically, which is why it is a great idea to try as many styles as you can. You will eventually find your own unique style if you watch as many varied dancers as you can and utilise their moves. Imitation is actually the key to developing your own style. Remember the bigger your style vocabulary, the more range you will have as a dancer. If you imitate and dance as many styles as you can, you will eventually find your own unique style that you are comfortable with.

Timing

Correct timing is essential for any dancer. Opinions vary on what is the best way to improve your timing. Most trained choreographers will encourage you to count and some will say that it is an absolute must. My opinion differs slightly. If you are training and practising for a piece, without accompaniment, then indeed, counting is essential and will help you keep form and improve progressively. Slow counting, out loud, gives you control and flexibility of pace as you practise. After rehearsal and practice is over though, I honestly feel that it is not necessary that you count in your head at all. As we have looked at earlier, you should almost put yourself in a state where the music flows through you. You already have your timing in the instruments. Let the snare and bass kick count for you. They are in effect metronomes; so why in addition to that would you need to count when you can trust the drums or percussion to do it quite effectively for you. Again, let the music flow through you and move with it as if you are one. A way to improve your timing is to become totally reliant on the music by becoming more familiar with it. It's surprising how much easier choreography and dancing become when you listen to the music and become an expert in the piece that you are dancing to. At the end of the day, it is the music which should dictate the physical movement, use it and its count as your metronome. If you don't have music, then count, but look at it as a temporary replacement of the music rather than a framework which you can't break out of, or a supplement to the music or song. Think about it, what's the difference between rhythm and counting and which is essential out of the two? You can indeed learn to count, but to have rhythm comes from inside you and your state and confidence as well as your connection to the music.

Control

Control of your body and movement is what dancing is all about and it is essential to master your body and movements so that you look good, stay injury free and move correctly. A dancer by definition should move in a controlled manner. Adrienne Leitch, in *Dance: Concise Definitions of Universal Dance Terms* puts it this way: "control – the ability to manage a variety of body actions with concentrated awareness of muscular activity in order to retain personal equilibrium." (Co-ordination) balance and control can be improved by firstly, moving slowly and secondly thinking slowly. Work methodically through each step with full consideration of poise, balance and where you intend to place your body. Other ways of improving your control are to work on your physical strength, especially your core strength and listen to the music and move with it. Think about what you are doing and execute each step in an intentionally slow way and with time you will begin to master your movement.

Placement and Accuracy

Speed is an essential part of dance, but NOT at the expense of accuracy and form. When the music is pumping and the blood is flowing it is easy to forget about your form and increase the tempo and energy you exert and put into a step. The opposite should be the case. The accents of a piece of music, for example, are enhanced by the accuracy and placement and not your speed, or the increased speed at the expense of control. In fact, speed will increase with your confidence after you have mastered a step, but not before.

So always start slow, master your step, focus on accuracy and placement, and when the music is turned up, stay relaxed and focussed rather than increase your speed or energy level. Your body posture and alignment is of utmost importance and it is essential that you remain focussed on that throughout dancing and performing. Focus on keeping your body upright and eyes level as well as letting the music hit the mark, dictating your movements. The faster you execute a step the more likely you are to miss your mark. It's essential that you think about your style, form, placement, control and accuracy if you want to dance well.

Simple Stretching

Stretching is important and is essential for any exercise or dance programme. You're stretching the muscle so that it is prepared and ready for exercise. Stretching can prevent the muscle from tightening up or shortening while in motion. This can be damaging to your health as well as significantly decreasing the range of your movements. Static stretches are stretches where you hold still, you should try and do as regularly as you can if you want to gently increase your flexibility. Try and hold each stretch for at least ten seconds, and no more than thirty seconds. It's also important that you stretch all of the muscle groups before and after you have worked out. Finally and most importantly, a stretch is not a suitable warm-up before physical activity! Warm up before you stretch. A good way to do this is to run on the spot for sixty seconds. If you don't warm up the muscle before you stretch, then you run the risk of damaging the filaments and the muscle itself. Here are four simple stretches to try:

Hamstring Stretch

Put both of your feet together. Bend both of your knees and extend one leg forward, while keeping the other leg bent. Place your hands on the top of your right thigh and lean forward from the hips. Make sure that you keep your abdominal muscles tight and hold for about fifteen seconds. To enhance this stretch, raise the toes of your extended leg. Now repeat with the opposite leg.

Figure 2: Hamstring Stretch

Front Thigh Stretch

You might want to get some stable support (like a chair or the side of a table). Start with your feet together and shift your weight onto one of your legs and soften the knee slightly. Raise the opposite leg (foot) up, toward your buttocks. Take hold of your ankle. Make sure that you keep your abdominal muscles tight and your knee facing the floor as well as your pelvis aligned and straight underneath you. Hold for fifteen seconds and then repeat with the other leg.

Figure 3: Front Thigh Stretch

Calf stretch

Take a chair, or stable support (like a table). Step forward with your back leg straight, in line with your back and your front leg, bent at the knee. Make sure that the back leg is completely straight with your heel pressed against the floor completely and that your hips are aligned forward too. Your toes should be facing forward and there should be a straight line from the top of your head, through your back and down your leg, to the floor.

Figure 4: Calf Stretch

Buttock Stretch

Hold your support and bend your supporting knee. Take the ankle of the opposite leg and bring it up in front of you and across the supporting leg. It should look like you're crossing your legs, in the air. Lean forward slightly from your waist, keeping your back straight, then relax and repeat with both legs.

Figure 5 Buttock Stretch

Feel Great, Have Fun

Okay, time for some child's play regarding the easiest way to feel great and stay in shape! It's really easy to change your outlook and feel great, and I'm going to let you into the secret. How to stay in shape, how to stay energised, how to just be well! Now, before I let you into the secret... I have to admit that I stole it, from probably the greatest actor ever: Marlon Brando. It's the secret weapon that I pull out when I'm feeling down or overworked.

As a choreographer and dance teacher, it's also my job to give advice on how much to dance and practise and exercise tips, But again, do you want to hear something that costs nothing and is so simple, that doesn't involve a fifteen-step plan and your hard earned cash, only a little determination? I always tell my students that the best way to stay healthy and keep fit is a) to dance and b) to run (although that's not the secret!). Trust me, I have heard every excuse conceivable in the book, why this is not possible. It's quite entertaining to hear the same excuses from so many different people! It's quite simple; although you might have to wake up forty-five minutes earlier in the morning. All you have to do is invest in a good quality pair of trainers (sneakers) and run daily... That's it! But of course, they would rather quote scientific theories on shock impact as if they're experts in Chondromalacia, Chronic exertional compartment syndrome, Great excuse syndrome as well as other knee disorders...Anything not to. To repeat Nike's words of wisdom: "Just Do It!"

It's really simple and is also the perfect way to jump into dance and any physical activity, especially for absolute beginners. Although it is very simple, it's something that so many people are unable to do. The number one way to lose weight and get into dance and get your backside moving! The bad news is that you won't want to hear it. It's probably too simple for you to accept!

The Secret

Marlon Brando. The man. Marlon Brando had the most amazing ability to lose weight. I mean, seriously, he would go from being a very healthy lean looking movie star to a massively overweight man, and then back again, in very short periods of time. But how? He was once asked in an interview, "How do you lose weight so quickly?" Now, you'd be surprised at his answer. Did it involve an army of Hollywood trainers? No! Did it involve subscribing to nonsensical unhealthy scam diets? No! It was completely free… and very easy to do. He would close the curtains, close the doors, put on a great piece of music full blast… and just go crazy! Yes, just move to the music. No choreography, no nothing! He said that he just copied the Hula dancers that he watched, with all that movement. You are a human being, with natural rhythm. Why do you need to learn to go enjoy a great happy song? You don't. And I mean, go crazy. Just do whatever you feel like, manoeuvre like a crazy beast. Just lose control for once. Feel free to lose your inhibitions and be free! Hey, nobody's watching, so who gives a damn anyway!

Marlon Brando filmed and vacationed in Hawaii, and was inspired and impressed by the natural movements, e.g. natural dance like the Samburu tribe dance, in Africa. Forget this nonsense that you have to learn how to do this, or learn how to do that or that you can only lose weight and keep fit and feel good with a yearly membership at the top gym, that you hardly attend anyway, repeating mechanical, totally unnatural, robotic movements in front of a flashing box. Which is a totally new phenomenon anyway. You tell me where the healthiest people in the world are. Not in the same locations as the countries with the most gyms, I bet!

As every philosopher has said, it's always a case of 'unlearning' rather than 'learning'. And one more thing, mentally, you will feel great afterwards too. For once, really do something spontaneous and give it a try! That is my personal feel-good keep fit advice: the technique that I employ when I'm feeling down. Now, as always, it might be too complicated for many people to do something so simple – but why not give it a try? It's the perfect place to start for a beginner and I guarantee that you'll feel great afterwards and really be in a better position to advance and learn, as well as keep in shape. My top five personally recommended songs are:

1. 'Le Freak' by Chic
2. 'Venus' by Bananarama
3. 'I Will Survive' by Gloria Gaynor

4. 'Manic Monday' by the Bangles
5. 'Puttin' on the Ritz' performed by Fred Astaire

Good luck! Think about your mental ability to try new things and not disregard something that may indeed help you. That simple thing might be something that you could use to progress. Don't disregard anything just because it sounds too simple. Advancement in the physical really does start in your head.

Dance Tricks and Gimmicks

Many of the most famous dancers and performers have captured the public imagination by utilising dance tricks or gimmicks. These are one of dance moves that get a crowd reaction.

Here are a few:

Spins
The Robot (robotics)
The Floss
The backslide and side slide (The Moonwalk)

These are used sparingly as a means of impact but can also be incorporated in a club or fun setting. Let's take a closer look at one... the backslide variation, the side slide! The backslide is a move which is a combination of floating, gliding and sliding, and has a more circular movement, which I like to call the "circle slide". Dancers like the legendary Jeffrey Daniel, who performed the backslide for years. Before that James Brown performed a kind of backslide. One of the most impressive backslides was performed in 1955 at the end of a tap sequence by the entertainer Bill Bailey.

The Side Slide

Just for fun! Let's give this a try!

Ideally, for this move you will need a smooth surface, comfortable trainers or any light shoes and comfortable clothes. Although it is ideal that you have a smooth surface to execute the side slide, it can be executed on carpet or pavement or any surface that doesn't have a substantially high amount of friction (like sand or mud, for example!). Pavement or less is fine. In fact, I suggest that you practise on a rougher floor first to get used to the mechanics of the steps and get used to pushing and transferring the weight into the floor so that it is easier when you want to perform or show off the move on the dance floor! The illusion of this move comes from the execution of the weight transfer, accurately, as opposed to the sliding which is why the moonwalk is classed as a "popping" move and not necessarily a "glide" as it may seem.

We are going to try and glide toward the side giving the illusion that we are floating on air, effortlessly. A glide is very much related to popping and is very similar to the backslide, but has more of an effortless, smooth quality to it. We will be using our feet to push, pull and turn to create the illusion. I like to call the step the "side slide" and it is one of my favourite steps, as it is quick and easy to perform after it has been mastered. Feel free to vary it and add your own interpretation and ideas to the move.

This is essentially a street dance step and consists of pretty unnatural body movements. Which adds to the illusion, as it looks like it is impossible to do, but only adds to the surreal effect. It's important to remember to learn one step at a time.

Firstly, break down the move and isolate each component; next master each one; and later join them together. Isolation is the key to this step; that is, moving different parts of your body independently of the rest. This requires focus and practice. But after a little practice, it becomes second nature - you'll start enjoying it once you've practised so much that you stop thinking about the steps, and just let your body go with the flow. As with every step or piece of choreography, try and allow the music to flow 'through' you as opposed to dancing 'on' the beat.

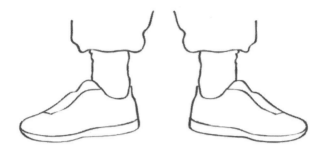

Figure 6 (i): Starting positioning of the feet (Side Slide)

One way of doing this is to literally imagine you are part of the music or an instrument in it, like a drum. Most important is practice and methodical conditioning. So let's have a closer look at the "side slide"...

Starting position: Stand with your back straight and your chin up. Place your feet shoulder width apart pointing diagonally outwards (See Figure 6).

- Bend your left leg at the knee and in the direction that your foot is pointing while raising your left heel off the floor. Keep your body up right and straight. You should feel the muscles in your left thigh working as they take your weight. It's important that you do not lean over. Keep your spine and upper body completely straight as you lower yourself into position.

- The pivot: You're now going to pivot on your left toe and right heel so that both of your toes are pointing inwards. Transferring your weight on to the left toe, swing your left heel toward the left. The position of your toes does not move, in relation to the floor.

At the same time, transfer the weight on your right foot, on your heel, swinging your toes in and to the left, raising your toes slightly off the floor. The heel of your right foot should not move its position in relation to the floor. Pivot both feet at the same time, with speed, keeping your back straight and your knees bent, as in the previous step.

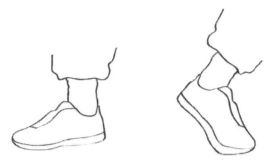

Figure 6 (ii): The Pivot (Side Slide)

Leg snap: Your left knee will be bent and your right straight. Snap your left knee back, and your right knee forward, so that this is reversed. Your right knee should push slightly toward the left at a diagonal and your left leg should snap toward the right at a diagonal. It's important that you keep your knees bent and back straight, as you will be tempted to straighten up. Keep the form of the first step throughout and keep low. When executing the leg snap, do not move any other part of your upper body (imagine an Elvis Presley shuffle!)

- Right angle: To prepare for the sliding motion you should turn your right heel in towards the other leg, while keeping your toe in contact with the floor. You might feel slightly unstable, temporarily, but it's important that you keep your form. Figure 6 (iii).

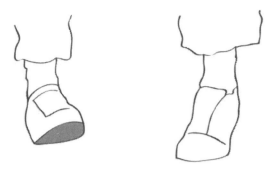

Figure 6 (iii)

- The slide: You are now going to use your right foot to slide to the left.

As you push off, turn your left foot in the direction that it is sliding and take the weight onto your left toes to stop the slide. When you push off the right foot, remember that you are to transfer equal weight off your right foot, into the left foot.

From there you should slide the foot into the floor and toward the left. You will create friction with the ground. It is that effort that will create the illusion that you are gliding. Remember to keep your back fully straightened and to transfer the weight through your legs and heels, in a snap. A "push, slide and snap (right heel down on the "snap")" motion. You might be tempted to raise up the toes of the left sliding foot, but keep them pushing into the floor and down at the same time as you slide toward the left in a swift sharp movement.

- The heel drag: Drag your right heel toward your left foot while pivoting on your left toes. Your heel should slide along and into the floor in a straight line (approx 20- 30 cm). When you pivot on the left foot, remember that the position of your toes do not change in relation to the floor and you are raising up, and swinging the left, your left heel simultaneously with the heel drag on the right foot.

-

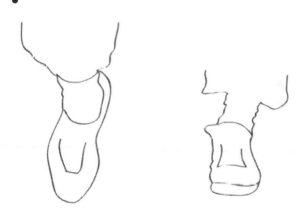

Figure 6 (iv) Heel Drag

- The toe flip: At the end of your heel slide, flip your right foot so that your toes are touching the floor and your heel is raised. Your foot should move in a swift movement, without moving in relation to the floor. You should imagine that you are pushing your right heel forward, while raising it, on the pointed foot. Keep it in, and tight while keeping the form of the rest of your body.

- Second slide: From this position you are now going to push off into another slide. Push down and into the floor with your right foot whilst sliding your left foot away. Remember to push your left toe in the direction you are travelling and keep your back upright and straight at all times. Also, keep in mind that it is an equal weight transfer via the floor! The friction and effort is a good thing, which you will get used to, but it is essential. If this is not an effort then you're sliding into the floor incorrectly and should push harder into the floor, so that it is!

Figure 6 (v)

- Heel drag: Repeat the heel drag as before by sliding your heel inward to the left while pivoting your left toe inwards. At the end of the movement flick your toes down and your heel up once more.

Join it up! You now have all the necessary footwork to pull the side slide off, but next, you have to join it up into one continuous line by accurately repeating the moves to build up speed and smoothness. It's important that before you attempt to join it up you master each step individually as well as focussing on isolating parts of your body. So that when you pivot (for example) the step has no effect on any other part of your body or your position or stance. Throughout this move (especially when learning the mechanics of the step) it's important to remember that the movements of the legs should not have any effect on your upper body or spine and that you should stay low and keep your body relative to the ground through the steps. It's also important that you master each step before attempting to join them up so that when you do join them up, it is a natural progression to the slide. At this stage, the weight transfers should be very mechanical and you should become very aware of your weight and where you are placing it through your body. The slide works because you are using weight transfer in a very unnatural way, which creates the illusion. It takes a while to get used to. With perseverance, you will get it!

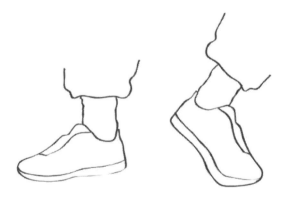

Figure 6 (vi)

The Upper Body

The arms: To complete the step add some upper body movement. Keep your arms straight and bring them to the front of your body with your fingers together pointing outwards and your palms parallel to the floor. Next, move your arms up and down from the shoulder. Add in a rotation so that your arms look like pistons driving the motion through the slide and the rest of your body. Do this at the same time as you are rotating to enhance the illusion.

Figure 6 (vii)

The head: Keep your back straight and make a circular movement in a clockwise direction with your head. Be careful not to jerk your neck, keeping the move smooth and steady. Really stretch your neck forwards, pushing your chin forward and down and then around in the circular motion. Focus on keeping your head completely straight, so that you do not tip in any direction. You can do this by keeping your eyes looking straight ahead and focussing on pushing the move with your chin and under neck area rather than your head. If you focus on your chin and under neck area, while still keeping your head upright, you'll be able to extend your head further forward and around in a clean simple motion, without it looking awkward.

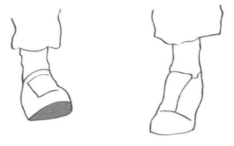

Figure 6 (viii)

Remember, practice makes perfect! The side slide needs a lot of practice to master, but if you put the effort in and focus on each step and try to understand the mechanics of the motion…you'll soon be busting the side slide everywhere!

There is no doubt that this seems like a complicated step, but with practice and training, it really does become second nature and a joy to perform and watch. As with most dance steps, there will be a certain point when it just feels right and it "clicks" into place (after practice). It may seem impossible before this point, but it is so important that you focus and keep going. It is a misconception that popping and locking are difficult and that only some people are able to do it. As with everything, if you break it down and practise each step slowly, then it will come together and in the end, you will be able to do it with accuracy and confidence.

Maintaining your Talent and Staying Well

The next few paragraphs are a summary of some of the things we have already looked at in detail, plus some new additions and tips. You may wish to incorporate these simple things into your lifestyle as they have the potential to transform your life and certainly improve your ability to dance and express your creativity.

Fitness

Fitness and exercise affect my feeling of wellbeing and ability to interact with the world. My usual exercise is running. I don't count my dancing as exercise because that's also a mental activity; I am usually teaching as well as moving. With running, I can just run. I used to run up to ten miles per day but I found, after a time, that this took too much out of me. So now I can run an hour pretty easily and still feel fresh and strong throughout the day. Exercise produces endorphins which lift our mood. I also see running as a social activity, even though I don't speak with anybody. I see people, I interact with them and this is a good thing because it reminds me that I am part of a wider society.

It goes without saying that any regular fitness activity will improve your self-confidence. If you incorporate a fitness routine, which you are comfortable with and enjoy, you will receive significant benefits to your outlook, mood, health and general wellbeing.

Sleep

When we're tired it doesn't help us interact with the world in a happy way. So it's important that you get enough sleep. How much sleep is a personal thing based upon your own body and your own activity. You want to sleep until you feel rested and then wake up. It's probably not a good thing to sleep for less than eight hours regularly but you should experiment and see what amount of rest helps you to feel best. For me, the way I am awoken is extremely important.

Get into a relaxed state prior to sleep – this might include not having a television or other screens on in the bedroom.

Food

We are what we eat and I have experimented for weeks with different diets and different foods and this is what I can report:

Sugar

Cutting sugar out will change your life. When I cut sugar out, I felt like a different person. My mood changed, as much as I became more patient and more tolerant. I also felt more energetic and more stable.

Processed Foods

I cut out processed foods and replaced them with, as best as I could, organic healthy real food. People commented how bright and vibrant I looked and I just felt more peaceful and that I could handle the world better. I can say that cutting all the processed stuff out completely transformed the way I felt for the better.

Milk and Meat

I found that I had to reduce my running from ten miles a day because my energy levels, without meat, were significantly lower until I replaced meat with fish. Cutting out the dairy also helped me feel better and fresher. You should experiment with what works for you. This may be without, meat or fish or milk, for example.

Incorporating all of the above

When I incorporated all of the above, I often described it as life-changing and feeling like a new human being. I felt that I was less emotional and less reactive. Experiment with what works for you. Whatever you consume, consume it consciously and take note of how you feel that day and the next day. If you need to keep a diary.

We've already looked at some possible options with regards to health, nutrition and fitness. Now we're going to look briefly at some other types of maintenance.

Meditation

I have meditated for many days consecutively. I can say with my hand on heart it has been life-changing. However, before I tell you about the specific meditation I do, I would encourage you, if you wish to meditate, to find one that you are comfortable with and works for you. You can look online or in books. Another thing you can do is just sit peacefully. Turn off the electric gadgets and phones as well as the lights and just sit for a few moments and be peaceful. You will be surprised how many ways this benefits you.

Another brilliant way of relaxing the brain is to find a peaceful meditative piece of music, say, Erik Satie's relaxing 'Gymnopedies' and again, turn off all the lights and gadgets and just sit and listen. I currently mediate for around forty minutes each day, however, I'm going to tell you about an easier one that I did for many days.

It's called 'Isha Kriya' from an Indian Yogi called Sadhguru. He looks the part. If you want a meditation you want one from a guy that looks like this! You can do a short thirteen minutes per day and it's in three parts. You just sit on a chair and essentially repeat (internally) to yourself, "I am not the body … I am not even the mind", then you make a certain sound, then you sit peacefully. You can find out more yourself online through the Isha Foundation or find an alternative meditation that may work for you. If you can find one then feel free to make one up!

Control surroundings and environment (recuperate and safe spaces)

It's very important that you create a safe space in your life where you can recuperate and relax without being disturbed, for an amount of time which you feel recharges your batteries. I would suggest that you do whatever you need to do to make it the best it can be. Fully soundproof a space if you must; just make sure that you have a place in your life to retreat to when things get too much.

If you can remove yourself from noise and disturbance then this is the best way – by creating distance. Or move if an environment really doesn't work. Don't be afraid of change as this will improve the quality of your life.

Get up to date medical attention and any psychological help

Make sure that you see the doctor regularly and keep up to date with your check-ups and medication. Also, do not be afraid to ask for any kind of psychological help you may need.

Cultivate human real world relationships with non-dancers

Remember that you must try as hard as you can to put time aside to cultivate real world friendships and relationships and invest in them. This is good for you but your friends can also help you in times of need. It's also important to keep the people around you diverse. I strongly advise you to make sure that you have a mixed bunch of friends and not just dancers and performers. Ironically, this will help you as a dancer and performer because they will help give you a different kind of perspective and view of the world.

FAQs

Should I apply for a dance school?

I strongly suggest that if you want to be a professional dancer a dance school will put you in contact with like-minded people and give you the training required. Ironically one of the main reasons to go to dance school and get a performing arts-based education is not only to learn the basics of your craft but also to experience the joys of being around people also want to express their creativity in a safe space where your personality can shine and you will have an opportunity to demonstrate your talent which is, what it's all about. It can also help you create a network of fellow dancers that can launch you directly into the professional world. For this reason, I strongly suggest that if possible, you attend a very good dance school. With that said it is not a requirement, you can succeed as a professional dancer without going to dance school. Some of the greatest dancers of all time didn't go to dance school and some didn't have formal dance training at all! Sometimes you can enter the industry directly but I strongly recommend that you do apply for a dance school because the probability of you becoming a professional dancer at a young age with no formal dance training is, relatively speaking, low… but nevertheless possible! If your stars are aligned and you have the talent you will make it regardless of formal training dance training or no training. In summary, I strongly recommend that you apply for a dance school if not to advance your dance ability and training but to advance you as a human being.

Is it best to start with a dance education or for professional experience first?

This depends on your set of circumstances for example if you need to ask this question my feeling is that you should start with your dance education first because the question in itself is answering the question. If you already are dancing professionally obviously you should continue on your path because it is already working out for you, however, if something is not working out for you then you should focus on training and dancing professionally simultaneously if need be. Statistically speaking I advise you to jump into formal dance training as soon as possible but whatever path you choose you can make work as there is no right or wrong way.

How long does it take to become a good dancer?

It varies depending on the abilities and the person that you are speaking to. Some people will take a very long time and some people will take no time at all, and then we need to look at what and how we define the word "good", too! For example, I was performing from the age of ten years old and I have danced professionally since them. On the other hand, some people might need their teenage years to grow into becoming a "good" dancer whilst others might need longer. I do think to be a professional dancer you do have to have, to *some* extent, a natural ability or strong drive which you then work on with training. By the time you are sixteen to eighteen years old, I would expect to see that talent manifest in some clear form.

Do you have to be flexible to dance?

It's not a requirement to particularly be flexible or to be able to do the splits, for example, to dance professionally. However, if you are not flexible you are severely restricting opportunities and there is no reason why you shouldn't be as that is part of what it is to be a dancer. With that said the truthful answer is that you do not have to be flexible to dance necessarily because you don't need anything to dance except a body and do what is required dependent on the particular style of moves you are doing. If flexibility is not required for what you are doing then it is simply not required and that is fine! However, working on your flexibility is very important not only for your dance ability but also for your health and wellbeing… it is unwise for a budding professional dancer to restrict their options and opportunities by neglecting your flexibility!

How long does it take to become a professional dancer?

I've heard a lot of statistics with regards to how long it takes to become a professional dancer from eight to ten years with dancers and students starting their training from the age of seven years old etc. However the bottom line is that it does not take any set amount of time to become a professional dancer! If you go to dance school you may train for three or five or more years and often times the dance schools have rules which will restrict you dancing professionally whilst you are in training and others will not. It's important to remember that you make your own path and your own rules! Do not ever allow anyone else to impose their timelines on your life story. However long it takes you to become a professional dancer is your choice at the end of the day depending on the path and the direction you take. It can be as short as no time at all, to ten years or more.

Should I work for free to gain experience?

This is an incredible question and a difficult one to answer but my gut instinct is to advise you not to ever work for free and to value your work. Why should you work for free? There is something which feels disrespectful about asking somebody to work for free unless it is for charity or another good cause. I do believe that many people and companies play on dancers' fears about not getting work by offering "free" work that they should be paying for. They find dancers that are essentially willing to do the work for free. So they are not incentivized to offer payments when there are dancers who would do it for free. Some of those dancers don't know that they deserve to be paid. I remember dancing with five other backing dancers at a restaurant bar opening and they promised us very little money and didn't even pay us that! In fact, they didn't even give us the drinks that they promised us. This happened when I was starting out as a dancer and it has given me a different perspective which is that some people will take advantage of you if they feel that they can and if I'm being really honest many people do not consider an artist's efforts as legitimate work so will often take advantage of the artist, because they don't consider what they do as work and have no respect for what the artist does.I would also add that I am in a slightly different position in that I had professional experience from such a young age that I did not value offers of "experience" given to me because I did not need it. Now the question is, what if you do not have experience? What I would say is that you can get the experience and be paid too! At the beginning of your career, as a compromise, you might be paid your expenses or to be paid something for your work because at the very least it is a sign of respect. Never allow people to control you and disrespect your talent by making you do something that you are not comfortable doing. When somebody asks you do something, the first question should be "How much are you paying?" A very good way of asking this, if you are shy is to ask, "What is your budget?" That will usually sort them out and put certain people off, because they will see that they can't take advantage of you. There are many people who will try and take advantage of you and your talent in the entertainment industry… enforce your boundaries and never be afraid or ashamed to do so!

How long is an average dancer's career?

This is an interesting question and I think that it's important to be positive and optimistic because the truth is that you can have a career in dance for almost your entire life. For example, a dancer called Sylvester, that I knew, who starred in the movie "Cleopatra" literally taught ballet well into his late seventies. So the natural progression from being a professional dancer is that of becoming a professional dance teacher which means that there is no "end date" as long as you are physiologically able to teach and to dance. With regards to your ability to be hired in the entertainment industry as a dancer, I would suggest that the options vary but might be comparable to that of an athlete and also your ability to keep injury free because ultimately if you are injured and can't dance that is the end of your career in dance. With that said, the progression can easily take you from being a professional dancer to being a choreographer and being a dance teacher so the options are open for you to continue in dance and the entertainment industry for almost your entire life if that's what you wish. Practically speaking in the pop world your optimum age range will be between the age of eighteen years old and thirty years old, however, ultimately it's up to you and your unique set of circumstances as to how long you can dance for.

Do I need to learn ballet to become a professional dancer?

I strongly advise you to learn, at the very least the basics of ballet so that you can become the best dancer that you can be and as versatile a dancer as you can be. If you don't do so you are restricting your skills and your ability to be hired as a dancer. With that said, it is not required to become a professional dancer.

How much money does a professional dancer earn?

Statistically speaking, few dancers will become rich and many dancers will probably earn almost minimum wage (or less) of around £15,000 to £20,000 per year. Some might earn £200 – £300 for a full day's work. This can increase drastically depending on your particular set of skills and talent. Some dancers can earn up to £1,000 per day and sometimes much more.

Is it ever too late to start dancing?

It is never too late to start dancing. It is also never too late to dance and to earn money from dancing.

What possibilities are there in dance?

If you turn on the television almost every other channel will incorporate some kind of dancing or be involved in the industry, from commercials to concerts and entertainment etc. So you have countless options, opportunities and possibilities with regards to dancing in plays, becoming a backing dancer at a concert, choreographing and becoming a dance teacher, getting involved with commercials or anything to do with the entertainment industry where your dance skills can be utilised are options for you. However, there are even more options including in health and fitness where you can dance for wellbeing and for health and fitness purposes where you may teach as a professional which means that you will be paid.

There are literally countless opportunities to work in the entertainment industry.

I live in the middle of nowhere what should I do?

I have taught many dance classes abroad in small rural communities (in some places with under 150 people in a village or town). However, it's important not to forget that nowadays you can learn virtually, in a variety of ways and expand your skills via say, DVD, for example, or by learning from what you see online, on television and also by reading books etc. This means that you can use your time wherever you are located to become the best that you can be. Sometimes living in this type of area can actually be advantageous to you! I'll give you an example. If you are the only person interested in teaching dance then potentially you could become the most well known dance teacher in that whole area and can build your reputation that way. On the other hand, if you feel that your options are restricted by an area and you have done everything that you can do to fulfil your potential in that area then consider moving somewhere residential with more options for you. Follow your heart and if you feel like you need to move to a new city or country to train, then do so. The experience in itself will be amazing for you as there is nothing more fulfilling than following your dream and doing something that you enjoy. In fact, there is no way that you can fail. Failing is to not follow your dream and live in regret. Aim to reach your full potential, firstly, where you are and once you have done so, to the best of your ability, feel free to move to a different location to continue your evolution and growth in dance.

Dance classes are very expensive what do I do?

I want to tell you a story a dancer friend of mine. She is an incredible dancer and I've worked with her for a very long time. There was a period of time where she was disillusioned by the dance world and she was finding it tough. She was spending a lot of money on daily dance classes and she wasn't getting the work from the agency who also ran her dance classes. I asked her to make a simple calculation; how much money have you earned from the agency from the jobs that they have given you, in the history of your association with them? I then asked her to calculate how many years she had been attending their dance classes and how many lessons she had paid for. I then asked her to tally it all up and to work out what the numbers were. She later called me, horrified! She hadn't realised that she had paid them thousands of pounds and had had a very small return which was in the few hundreds of pounds. That translated, to her as a loss of tens of thousands of pounds. She realised that she was paying thousands of pounds to express her talents in someone else's class, for their benefit and essentially enriched them. I was so happy that she saw the transactional nature and the reality of the situation that she was in. Sometimes you should look at your life logically in this way. If you are spending thousands of pounds on dance classes and giving that money to an agency and that agency gives you a very minute about back then you are enriching them for no benefit to yourself and you should stop immediately. Invest your money where it is valuable for you and you can be in enriched and rewarded rather than enriched others. Sometimes dance agencies and even certain dance teachers play on your fears and manipulate you to pay them with the promise of work that never arrives. Never fall for this trick because if you are good enough you should be used based on your talent and merits, regardless if you attend someone's dance classes or not. Don't allow people to manipulate you and to use your talent to enrich them. Be strong, be confident and be proud of your abilities you will succeed if you work hard. Good luck!

Source Notes

Dance like the stars by Anthony King (2007)

The Personal Development Book for Performers (2019)

Bernstein, Richard, Dr.Bernstein's Diabetes Solution: Complete Guide to Achieving Normal Blood Sugars, Little, Brown & Company, 2004

Bilous, Dr. Rudy W, The British Medical Association Family Doctor Guide to Diabetes, Dorling Kindersley Publishers, 1999

Brzezinski, Zbigniew, Between Two Ages: America's Role in the Technetronic Era, Greenwood Press, 1982

Covey, Sean, 7 Habits of Highly Effective teenagers, Franklin Covey Co, 1998

Cummins, Stephen, Fibonacci Sequence, Xlibris Corporation, 2005

Dumas, Alexandre, The Count of Monte Cristo, Penguin Classics, republished 1997

Ellmann, Richard, Oscar Wilde, Vintage, 1988

Hill, Napoleon, Think and Grow Rich, Ballantine
    Books, 1987
Leitch, Adrienne, Dance: concise definitions of
    universal dance terms, Victoria, 2000
Philips, Bill, Body for Life, Collins, 1999
Wilde, Oscar, The Complete Works of Oscar
    Wilde: Volume 1, Poems and Poems in
Prose, Oxford University Press, 2000
Special thanks to Mr Mohammed Nabulsi
    (MRPharmS) Member of the Royal
Pharmaceutical society of Great Britain for being
    my nutritional advisor on this book (2007)

The History of dance

https://www.preceden.com/timelines/34962-
    history-of-dance
http://www.historyworld.net/timesearch/default.a
    sp?conid=timeline&getyear=-
    10000000&keywords=%20%20%20Dance
https://www.streetswing.com/histmain/d5timlne.
    htm
https://en.wikipedia.org/wiki/History_of_dance
https://blog.steezy.co/most-important-dance-
    terms/
https://en.wikipedia.org/wiki/Glossary_of_dance_
    moves

https://www.contemporary-dance.org/dance-terms.html

https://ballethub.com/ballet-terms-dictionary/

The Dancing Brain: Structural and Functional Signatures of Expert Dance Training (by Agnieszka Z. Burzynska, Karolina Finch, Brittany K. Taylor, Anya M. Knecht and Arthur F. Kramer) in Frontiers in Human Neuroscience

Agnieszka Burzynska, interviewed by Galadriel Watson, Dance magazine – dancemagazine.com (9th January 2018)

Diane Solway, in her fascinating New York Times (May 28th 2007) How the body (and mind) learns a dance

Dance and the brain

https://neuro.hms.harvard.edu/harvard-mahoney-neuroscience-institute/brain-newsletter/and-brain-series/dancing-and-brain

https://www.dancemagazine.com/dancers-brains-2523641417.html

https://www.helsinki.fi/en/news/health/a-dancers-brain-develops-in-a-unique-way

Hanna Poikonen @WiseMotionCo

https://www.nicabm.com/brain-parkinsons-disease-and-dance-55491/

https://www.psychologytoday.com/us/blog/the-athletes-way/201310/why-is-dancing-so-good-your-brain

Hanna Poikonen, A dancer's brain develops in a unique way (30th August 2018) helsinki.fi

Scott Edwards article Dancing and the Brain for Harvard Medical School on neuro.hms.harvard.edu and 2012 study by researchers at North Dakota's Minot State University

Effects of dance on motor functions, cognitive functions, and mental symptoms of Parkinson's disease: A quasi-randomized pilot trial. Complementary Therapies in Medicine, April 2015 by Hiroko Hashimoto (Hashimoto, Takabatake, Miyaguchi, Nakanishi, Naitou)

Dance timeline, vocabulary and styles explained

http://www.historyworld.net/wrldhis/PlainTextHistories.asp?historyid=ab82

https://en.wikipedia.org/wiki/History_of_dance

https://www.centralhome.com/ballroomcountry/history.htm

https://www.preceden.com/timelines/34962-history-of-dance

https://www.contemporary-dance.org/dance-history.html

Massive Attack, Angel (YouTube Official) https://www.youtube.com/watch?v=hbe3CQamF8k

Robinson737 https://www.youtube.com/channel/UCwqXV1DF-wbX2XfY8FwVPPw

https://massiveattack.ie/info/angel

Facing your Fears (a PERSPECTIVE NEUROSCIENCE article – Science 15 Jun 2018: Vol. 360, Issue 6394, pp. 1186-1187 DOI: 10.1126/science.aau0035)

By Paul W. Frankland and Sheena A. Josselyn in Science magazine

'Why Science Says It's Okay to Give Up on Your Music Career Goals' By Anthony Cerullo from the sonicbids blog

http://blog.sonicbids.com/why-science-says-its-okay-to-give-up-on-your-music-career-goals

https://www.forbes.com/sites/modeledbehavior/2015/12/31/sorry-george-lucas-but-star-wars-proves-the-profit-motive-can-be-good-for-art/

Geroge Lucas, Forbes interview (31st December 2015), by Adam Ozimek

Mike Fleming Jr, in a deadline.com, interview Geroge lucas (December 18, 2015):

'Star Wars' Legacy II: An Architect Of
Hollywood's Greatest Deal Recalls How
George Lucas Won Sequel Rights
https://deadline.com/2015/12/star-wars-franchise-
george-lucas-historic-rights-deal-tom-pollock-
1201669419/
'Francis Ford Coppola: Promises to Keep' by
Robert Lindsey, New York Times article (July
24th 1988)
https://www.nytimes.com/1988/07/24/magazine/
francis-ford-coppola-promises-to-keep.html
Business Insider, by Matthew Michael reported
(May 2018):
https://www.businessinsider.my/rich-famous-
celebrities-who-lost-all-their-money-2018-5/
Dance like the stars by Anthony King (2007)
The Personal Development Book for Performers
(2019)

The Psychology of Auditions

https://www.backstage.com/magazine/article/boo
king-ratios-1-58974/
backstage.com 2010 "Booking Ratios" by 'secret
agent man'
Cecilia Capuzzi Simon's New York Times April
2008 article "Try-outs for the Rest of Your Life"

https://www.nytimes.com/2008/04/20/education/
    edlife/theater.html
The Personal Development Book for Performers
    (2019)

Dance

https://www.hopkinsmedicine.org/health/conditio
    ns-and-diseases/sports-injuries/common-
    dance-injuries-and-prevention-tips
https://www.trinitylaban.ac.uk/student-
    life/student-support/health-injury-
    support/dance/injury-advice
Paul W. Frankland and Sheena A. Josselyn,
    Science magazine, Facing your Fears (a
    PERSPECTIVE NEUROSCIENCE article –
    Science 15 Jun 2018: Vol. 360, Issue 6394,
    pp. 1186-1187 DOI:
    10.1126/science.aau0035)
Anthony Cerullo, 'Why Science Says It's Okay to
    Give Up on Your Music Career Goals' from
    sonicbids blog
The International Association for Dance
    Medicine & Science (www.iadms.org)
    resource page by Nadia Sefcovic, DPT,
    COMT and Brenda Critchfield, MS, ATC
    under the auspices of the Education

Committee of IADMS

Stretching Scientifically: A Guide to Flexibility
    Training 4th Edition by Thomas Kurz

Dance like the stars by Anthony King (2007)

The Personal Development Book for Performers
    by Anthony King(2019)

Sadhguru Meditation:
    https://www.ishafoundation.org/Ishakriya

A closer look at some of the greatest dancers and choreographers of all time

Astaire Dancing – The Musical Films by John
    Mueller (1986 – Alfred A. Knopf)

Fayard Nicholas interview USA Today (2005) –
    Published 1/25/2006

www.waderobson.com

Josephine Baker Official Website:
    https://www.cmgww.com/stars/baker/

https://www.biography.com/performer/fred-
    astaire

https://en.wikipedia.org/wiki/Fred_Astaire

https://en.wikipedia.org/wiki/Gene_Kelly#Stage_
    career

https://www.biography.com/performer/gene-kelly

https://www.imdb.com/name/nm0000037/

https://www.britannica.com/topic/Nicholas-

Brothers
https://en.wikipedia.org/wiki/Nicholas_Brothers
http://www.nicholasbrothers.com/
https://www.britannica.com/biography/Mikhail-
    Baryshnikov
https://www.imdb.com/name/nm0000864/
https://www.imdb.com/name/nm0000237/
https://en.wikipedia.org/wiki/John_Travolta
http://travolta.com/
https://en.wikipedia.org/wiki/Michael_Flatley
https://www.michaelflatley.com/
https://en.wikipedia.org/wiki/Rudolf_Nureyev
https://nureyev.org/rudolf-nureyev-
    biography/main-dates-of-his-life/
https://www.imdb.com/name/nm0002080/
https://www.britannica.com/biography/Bob-Fosse

Health, Fitness and Nutrition

https://www.nutrition.org.uk/
https://www.nutrition.org.uk/healthyliving/health
    issues/tips-for-a-healthy-heart.html
https://www.nutrition.org.uk/healthyliving/health
    ydiet.html
https://www.nutrition.org.uk/healthyliving/health
    ydiet/healthybalanceddiet.html
https://www.nhs.uk/live-well/eat-well/

https://www.nhs.uk/live-well/eat-well/#food-groups-in-your-diet

https://www.nhs.uk/live-well/eat-well/#eat-less-saturated-fat-sugar-and-salt

https://www.nhs.uk/live-well/eat-well/#starchy-foods-in-your-diet

https://ukhealthcare.uky.edu/university-health-service/health-education/nutrition

https://www.hhs.gov/fitness/resource-center/facts-and-statistics/index.html

https://health.gov/dietaryguidelines/

https://www.usda.gov/topics/food-and-nutrition

https://www.nal.usda.gov/fnic/nutrition-and-health-organizations

https://www.nal.usda.gov/fnic/fitness-and-sports

https://www.nal.usda.gov/fnic/food-and-nutrition

https://www.nutrition.gov/

https://molechex.com.au/index.php/about-us/

https://www.amazon.com/Dr.-Mileham-Hayes/e/B01M0ULWXN%3Fref=dbs_a_mng_rwt_scns_share

Skin Cancer, Melanoma and Mimics by Dr. Mileham Hayes

Practical Skin Cancer Surgery published by Elsiver by Dr. Mileham Hayes

Special Thanks

Dr Cho Cho Khin
Karsten, Hege, Kasper and Taran
Mohammed Nabulsi
Rolfe Klement (Creative Sunshine back cover
photography)
Debz Hobbs-Wyatt
Aimee Coveney
Jason and Marina
Sam Perera
Shivy Gohil (illustrations)
Clair Challinor
Jordan Cather

About the Author

Anthony King is a choreographer who started teaching dance at the world-famous Pineapple Dance Studios, London in 2004 and has authored seven books on a variety of subjects, from Dance to Asperger's to Music History. He has taught stars from music, sport and film including Emma Watson, Miss World, Harry Potter, various members of royalty (European and Middle Eastern), Pink Floyd, *Top of the Pops*, *The Jonathan Ross Show*, *Richard and Judy Show*, *Britain's Got Talent*, BBC's *EastEnders*, BBC's *The Office*, and the England football team. Choreographed fashion shows for Vidal Sassoon, Anthony has starred in and choreographed commercials for Sony PlayStation, Maverick Media, Warner Music and more. Anthony is the original choreographer of the west end musical, *Thriller Live*. Anthony has held dance team building events and workshops for the world's biggest companies from Twitter to Google, HM

Treasury Department, Lego, Capgemini, Anglo American, PwC, Bonnier Publishing, King (creators of Candy Crush), City Sprint, Red Bull, Cisco Systems, TK Maxx, American Express, Proctor & Gamble, Metro Newspaper group, Rimmel London and many more. He has been interviewed on most of the world's national and international media including Sky News, BBC News, BBC Breakfast, Channel 4, Channel 5, ITV, ITV 2, CNN, ITN, BBC Radio 1, Capital FM, Choice FM, BBC Radio London and many more. His online lessons have been viewed over 35 million times as well as being featured on YouTube homepage on numerous occasions. His classes have been described by *The Sun* newspaper as 'Hot!' *Elle* magazine have featured his classes as the 'NEXT BIG THING' as well as "dynamic and charismatic" by the *London Lite*. *The Financial Times* of London has recommended and featured Anthony's classes and he has been featured as a contributing writer for magazines including *More!* magazine as 'Celebrity dance tutor'.

Anthony King's Online Consultations

If you'd like to contact Anthony personally with regards to personal online consultations for help, advice or just to talk about any subject from this book please email: info@anthony-king.com or see **www.anthony-king.com** for more details.

Also by the Author

Living in a Bubble: A Guide to being diagnosed
with High Functioning Asperger's as an Adult

The Personal Development Book For Performers

Michael Jackson Fact Check –
Fact checking the Michael Jackson 'experts'

Michael Jackson and Classical Music

Anthony King's Guide to
Michael Jackson's Dangerous Tour

Anthony King's Guide to
Michael Jackson's HIStory Tour

Dance Like The Stars

Made in the USA
Middletown, DE
25 May 2021